Geography

D1029709

Economic Development in Latin America

PRAEGER SPECIAL STUDIES IN
INTERNATIONAL ECONOMICS AND DEVELOPMENT

Economic Development in Latin America

AN ANNOTATED BIBLIOGRAPHY

John R. Wish
Department of Marketing
Michigan State University

FREDERICK A. PRAEGER, Publishers
New York · Washington · London

Universitas
BIBLIOTHECA
Ottaviensis

The purpose of the Praeger Special Studies is to make specialized research monographs in U.S. and international economics and politics available to the academic, business, and government communities. For further information, write to the Special Projects Division, Frederick A. Praeger, Publishers, 111 Fourth Avenue, New York, N.Y. 10003.

FREDERICK A. PRAEGER, PUBLISHERS
111 Fourth Avenue, New York 3, N.Y., U.S.A.
77-79 Charlotte Street, London W.1, England

Published in the United States of America in 1966
by Frederick A. Praeger, Inc., Publishers

Second printing, 1966
All rights reserved

© 1965 by John R. Wish

Library of Congress Catalog Card Number: 65-21105

Printed in the United States of America

Z
7165
.L3W5
1965

FOREWORD

A good bibliography is not unlike a good newspaper, full of very local and very timely information which does get dated and is never finished. This bibliography is tightly focused because it was prepared in connection with a sizable research program about food marketing in Latin America that is just now getting under way. Mr. Wish has been one of the key contributors to the planning of this larger project. Not the least of his contributions is this bibliography.

This annotated bibliography is a view into an ongoing process reporting one of the great economic, social, and political revolutions of modern times. It has the particular merit of blending the perspectives (and listing the literature) of three major streams of research which unfortunately do not often overlap. Agriculture research has a rich tradition covering both technical and economic factors. Communications is a new field bringing different methods and concepts to the problems of economic development. Finally, marketing is the most recent of these three approaches to develop a systematic literature dealing with economic development. It is no accident that Mr. Wish blends the three approaches to economic development. His initial graduate training and continuing interest has been in the diffusion of innovations working at the Ohio State University with Dr. Everett Rogers. Mr. Wish continues that work in marketing here at Michigan State University.

The history of a work often tells the reader much about it, including its strengths and limitations. This work began as part of the research efforts of Michigan State's Food Marketing Program to improve food marketing efficiency in developing areas of the world. The International Center of the University contributed to the support of the research and planning which led to this publication as well as the major project now being initiated, a two-and-one-half year United States Agency for International Development-sponsored study of food marketing efficiency in Latin America. The study is to be conducted jointly by Michigan State and the University of Puerto Rico.

Since food companies have been among the most active of American firms in Latin America, we feel they should have a special interest in this bibliography as well as the larger study.

The bibliography has merit, too, for other business readers and researchers interested in Latin America and/or the process of development.

Charles C. Slater
Michigan State University
Food Marketing Program

April, 1965

AUTHOR'S PREFACE

Introduction

Although this annotated bibliography was prepared primarily to assist Michigan State University staff members in a specific project,[1] I believe that a wide range of social scientists who are interested in Latin America will find it useful. The philosophical impetus for this bibliography lies in several of the recent speeches of Walter W. Rostow, who is presently the Chairman of the Policy Planning Council in the Department of State.

In a speech in late 1963, Dr. Rostow laid out several of his ideas regarding the "national market." He suggests that it is critical to the development process that more persons be brought into the money economy. Even the most lowly peasant should be able to sell some of his surplus food from his garden for money, so that he in turn can buy relatively inexpensive items such as shoes and bicycles. Dr. Rostow has further amplified his ideas in his most recent book, <u>View from the Seventh Floor</u>.[2] There he argues that more emphasis needs to be placed upon the production and distribution of goods that can be sold to peasants throughout the country. He believes that advice about markets and marketing can have a significant influence upon a nation's economy. In short, he argues that if processors and retailers begin

---

[1]That project concerns the role of food distribution in economic development. As submitted by the University's Latin American Studies Center to the United States Agency for International Development, it involves persons from the Colleges of Agriculture, Business, and Communication. The directors of the project are Dr. John T. McNelly, Dr. Harold M. Riley and Dr. Charles C. Slater. They will be concerned with communications, innovation and economic structure in food distribution systems of certain burgeoning urban areas of Latin America. Since it is hoped that most of the research for this USAID-financed project will be conducted in Puerto Rico and Colombia, there are a number of citations to those areas in this bibliography.

[2]See Item 3222 in the text of the bibliography for the complete citation of this book.

thinking about high volumes and low per-unit profits, the economy will grow faster.

<u>Organization of the Bibliography--How to use it</u>

In order to conserve space and prevent confusing the reader, each item is cited only once. I have attempted to list those items that apply to more than one area at the end of each applicable section. There the reader will find a listing which is prefaced by the statement, "See Also . . ." Thus, although each item is listed in the text only once, the item number may be given in the "See Also" list in a number of sections of primary interest.

Each item is identified by a four-digit number. <u>The first digit</u> indicates the chapter in which the item is listed. These six chapters were determined by the areas of interest and will be discussed in detail. <u>The second digit</u> indicates the section heading for <u>all items</u>. Its meaning remains constant throughout the bibliography and is as follows:

_0=Miscellaneous	_6=Statistics
_1=Area Studies	_7=Social Change
_2=Economic Development	_8=Other
_3=Marketing	_9=Bibliography
_4=Agriculture	
_5=Invention, Innovation and Entrepreneurship	

<u>The third and fourth digits</u> signify the item number beginning with 01 within each section <u>except</u> in the following instances: in Chapter 1--Series 1100 and 1150; Chapter V--Series 5500 and 5550, and Chapter VI--Series 6810, 6830, and 6870, the third digit is used to separate related but different areas. In these particular cases the third digit has arbitrarily been chosen to separate these related areas. With this brief explanation of the coding system for items, a closer look at the chapter delineations is desirable.

The first chapter is a compilation of items of primary interest to those scholars who do not yet have an extensive background in the issues of development. In the second chapter are items that deal with economic development in a more specific way. This chapter will be mainly of interest to those concerned with economics. In chapters three, four, and five are most of the items that apply especially to the USAID food marketing project. These three areas of marketing, communication and agriculture have much to do with development. They are not usually integrated in one context or focus as we do in this bibliography. Chapter Six gives the reader a look at some of the writings and issues involved in social science research. Particularly, the problems and opportunities of research in some of the developing nations such as those in Latin America are noted.

In order to be of greater help to the reader there are two appendixes. Appendix A is a short listing of information sources that proved helpful to me in making this bibliography. I became acquainted with most of the organizations and books listed in that appendix through professional librarians. However, I found these items one by one when, by chance, I asked the right question. This appendix may save some shoe leather of other researchers. It will likely be especially helpful to persons not intimately familiar with the inner workings of research libraries.

Appendix B, on the other hand, is a shortened bibliography. About ten percent of the items in the text have been indicated by a star (*) as being especially relevant. (I have made a value judgment and would suggest such items be among the first read.) All starred items are listed in numerical order by item number, author, and shortened title. If time is at a premium, go to Appendix B first.

Finally, items are indexed by author.

How the Bibliography was brought together

When the project, which Dr. Slater mentions in the foreword, was first being discussed in early 1964, there was a lack of knowledge of published reports of previous studies which might have a bearing on a food distribution project such as we contemplated. Dr. Slater and Dr. Riley asked that a bibliography be constructed. They set some broad parameters which are noted in the next section under the title "Criteria for Selection." Since I did not have the necessary breadth or time to do the entire work myself, I asked the assistance of some other persons.

Carl Eicher and William Miller had prepared an annotated bibliography in multilith for use of graduate students in an Agricultural Economics course here at Michigan State. Much of their material on marketing of food products in developing nations is included here. Gordon Whiting contributed a substantial number of the items in the methodology section and Kelly Harrison is responsible for many of the items concerning Puerto Rico.

The bibliography itself was started first by searching recent volumes of that excellent work which is edited by Earl J. Pariseau of the Library of Congress, The Latin American Studies Handbook.[3] Dr. Pariseau himself made several helpful suggestions for further additions to this bibliography. In early summer 1964, I made a five-day trip to Washington to search for materials not available in the Michigan State Library. Several of the theses noted in this bibliography were found in the microfilm section of the Library of Congress.

The compilation of this bibliography would have been very difficult without the helpful suggestions and ideas of Michigan State University Librarians such as Miss Eleanor Boyles (Documents Librarian), Mrs. Mary Berchan and Dr. Eugene DeBenko (International Library Librarians) and Mr. William Luft (Social Science Librarian). They opened my eyes to the vast amount of information and the publications already available. Some of the secondary source materials which a new social scientist might well search are listed in the section "Other Sources of Information."

In August, 1964, a first draft consisting of 339 items was mimeographed. Over two hundred copies of that edition, which was titled "A Selected Bibliography on Latin America with Particular Reference to Agriculture, Economic Development, and Marketing," were mailed to authors and others known to be interested in the areas noted. The recipients were asked for suggestions, criticisms and comments. As a result of numerous replies, an annotated and revised

[3] See Item 2910 in the text for the complete citation.

version of 414 items was given limited distribution in late January, 1965. Two persons were especially helpful in improving the first draft and should be noted here. Miss Barbara Heizman of the Technical Assistance Information Clearing House in New York gave many useful and helpful suggestions. Then too, Dr. George W. Westcott of the Economic Development Branch, United States Department of Agriculture, sent a gracious letter of five pages of suggested additions to the first draft. His on-the-spot experience in foreign agriculture was of great help in making the bibliography more meaningful.

Three persons were responsible for revisions to the January,1965,edition. Mrs. Mary Berchan, the Michigan State University Latin American Specialist, commented upon the bibliography as a Latin Americanist. Several of her suggestions are included. A former student of mine, Mr. John Mueller, read the January manuscript as an interested but uninformed reader. His comments and ideas were most helpful. In addition, he made the first attempt at cross-referencing of items. Then too, my wife, Mary Ann, made significant contribution, above and beyond that of spending many nights alone. It was she who did most of the checking of items for accuracy of the bibliographical information. She proofread the manuscript, she corrected my English. It is for these services that her name appears as a special assistant.

Finally, I owe a special thanks to three persons. The first is Mr. E. Lee Feller, a businessman and consultant in Coldwater, Michigan. It was Mr. Feller who first interested me in the role that business can play in economic development. He told me of his experiences in food distribution in Puerto Rico in helping implement the Galbraith and Holton report[4] in the mid-1950's. He introduced me to some of the more recent statements of W.W. Rostow. Mr. Feller is yet today a strong believer in the idea that changes in food distribution in the developing nations can materially contribute to economic development. Then too, I owe special thanks to Dr. Charles C. Slater, who has encouraged me in this work over

---

[4]See item 3122 in this bibliography.

the past year. The Michigan State University Food Marketing Program, which he directs, has made some financial contributions to this study. This study was also supported (in part) by the Michigan State University International Programs Ford Foundation grant, Latin American Studies Center.

Were it not for the encouragement, helpful suggestions, and stimulating atmosphere provided by Drs. Slater and Riley, this bibliography would not be. Still, the usual disclaimers apply. I would appreciate suggestions, criticisms and/or comments from any reader.

John R. Wish
Michigan State University

May, 1965

CRITERIA FOR SELECTION

of items in this bibliography

1. They are reasonably current (i.e., in most cases published since 1955).
2. They are relevant to the objective of operationalizing Rostow's "National Market" concept.
3. They may include some unpublished materials which are in process.
4. The bibliography must be kept to a reasonable number of items. Thus, none of the sections can list all the items published in a given area. This is a selected bibliography which is not meant to duplicate extensive bibliographies in specialized fields. However, some of those more specialized bibliographies are noted in the particular sections of this publication.

CONTENTS

CHAPTER 1 ORIENTATION

1100 SERIES

1100. The Less Developed Nations

1101. FEINSTEIN, Otto (ed.). Two Worlds of Change, Readings in Economic Development. Garden City: Doubleday-Anchor, 1964. 420 pp.

Feinstein has collected an unusual set of readings including such authors as Simon Kuznets, Adam Smith, Karl Marx, and W.W. Rostow.

D.B. Fusfeld, who wrote Chapter 3, "Economic Theory Misplaced: Livelihood in Primitive Society," concludes his article by saying that modern economic theory has two drawbacks in cross-cultural studies: "The categories and definitions of modern economics are not applicable to cross-cultural studies . . . . Secondly, the formal economics of maximization and allocation principles--the theory of choice--represents only a portion of the subject matter of economics . . . . The real task is nothing less than the building of a cross-cultural economics based on the substantive problems of production and distribution rather than on the formal problems of choice."

1102. LEWIS, Oscar. Pedro Martinez: A Mexican Peasant and His Family. New York: Random House, 1964. 534 pp.

This is a powerful human document. Reality

is presented through the eyes of a citizen of one of the less developed nations. Professor Lewis, who wrote The Children of Sanchez, has written a hard-hitting book that is a shocking description of the tenuous state of life of a peasant.

1103. MARCHANT, Pierre. "A Colombian Peon Tells His Moving Story," Realités, 142:65-68, September, 1962.

Most farmers in Latin America lead a primitive life and their fight for survival against hunger and disease absorbs all their strength. This is the story of one such peasant living in the Andes mountains isolated from the cities.

1104. SHONFIELD, Andrew. The Attack on World Poverty. New York: Vintage Books, 1962. 269 pp.

This book picks up where Barbara Ward leaves off. Shonfield gives specific suggestions for improving effectiveness of aid. The book has some very good sections interspersed with ones that aren't so useful.

1105. U.S. Army Area Handbook for Brazil. (Department of the Army Pamphlet No. 550-20.) Prepared by Foreign Area Studies Division, Special Operations Research Office, The American University. Washington, D.C.: U.S. Government Printing Office, July, 1964. (See also item 2112.)

This is another in the continuing series of orientation books on specific countries. The Army has contracted with the American University for the preparation of these studies. These unclassified handbooks provide an excellent introduction to the person who wishes to learn more of a particular country. (See also Area Handbook for Colombia.)

1106. *WARD, Barbara. The Rich Nations and The Poor Nations. New York: Norton, 1962. 159 pp.

The book is based upon lectures first given on the Canadian Broadcasting Corporation. It is a polemic on why we in rich western nations must be concerned, and why we must help the poorer nations.

Other items that deal with an Orientation to the Less Developed Nations are:

1151, 1153, 1155, 1204, 1209, 1701, 1707,
1712, 2006, 2008, 2015, 2017, 2104, 2114, 2117,
2807, 2904, 2909, 3005, 3105, 3108, 3110, 3113,
3115, 3133, 3137, 3139, 3146, 3156, 3202, 3205,
3214, 3217, 3401, 3408, 3409, 4001, 4006, 4008,
4101, 4103, 4108, 4115, 4202, 4209, 4904, 5006,
5009, 5511, 5556, 5702, 5709, 5722, 5801, 5806,
5807, 5812, 5814, 5902, 6009, 6011, 6023, 6601,
6603, 6609, 6618, 6622, 6818, 6873.

1150. <u>Latin America</u>

1151. AREVALO, Juan J. <u>The Shark and the Sardines</u>. Translated by June Cobb and Raul Osequeda. New York: Lyle Stuart, 1961. 256 pp.
The U.S. is depicted as Uncle Shark feeding upon the little sardines--Latin America. This is not the kind of description an American likes to read, but it is one with which he should be familiar.

1152. BRANDENBERG, Frank. <u>The Development of Latin American Private Enterprise.</u> (Planning Pamphlet #121.) Washington: National Planning Association, 1964. 136 pp. Bibliographical footnotes.
In the author's preface one reads, "The purpose of this study is to assess the means by which private enterprise in Latin America can increase its contribution to the area's economic, political and social progress . . . " The study is in six parts. Brandenberg attempts to study the setting of private business; the persons who make it up; relations with their government; the importance of foreign investments; and finally he suggests ways to strengthen private enterprise. Though his conclusions and recommendations are necessarily general, the study is well worth reading.

1153. DRUCKER, Peter F. "A Plan for Revolution in Latin America," <u>Harper's</u>, 222:31-38, July, 1961.
Drucker suggests some ways in which sound reform programs can and should be brought about.

1154. EISENHOWER, Milton S. <u>The Wine is Bitter: The United States and Latin America</u>. Garden City: Doubleday, 1963. 342 pp.
The neophyte who wishes to learn of Latin Americans and their feelings, problems and attitudes would do well to start with this book. Eisenhower says that there are real reasons why troubles exist in

many places throughout the Southern Hemisphere. In his concluding chapter he suggests that the choice today is "between a peaceful but revolutionary alliance for progress and bloody revolution."

1155. *HIRSCHMAN, Albert O. (ed.). Latin American Issues: Essays and Comments. New York: Twentieth Century Fund, 1961. 201 pp.

Little effort has been taken on our part to understand Latin America. This is an effort to foster understanding. The essays have been written by authors from various countries. An essential book for those who wish to understand Latin American development.

1156. HOLT, Pat M. Colombia Today-And Tomorrow. New York: Praeger, 1964. 209 pp. Bibliography.

The book is mainly based upon newsletters written by the author while in residence in Bogota in 1961-62. It is primarily a study of the country, its opportunities and its problem. A good book for background.

1157. MEDINA-E., Josc, and HIGGINS, Benjamin. Social Aspects of Economic Development in Latin America. Vol. II Paris: UNESCO, 1963. 272 pp.

The text is based on the proceedings of a conference of the same title.

1158. NEHEMKIS, Peter. Latin America: Myth and Reality. New York: Alfred A. Knopf, 1964. 286 pp.

The author ranges over a wide span of current issues such as agrarian reform, industrialization, political development, and economic integration. He poses some hard questions regarding such topics as representative governments and the role of the businessman. (See Powelson for a similar approach.)

1159. VRIES, Egbert de, and MEDINA-E., Jose (eds.) Social Aspects of Economic Development in Latin America. Vol. 1 Paris: UNESCO, 1963. 401 pp.

Papers on the social aspects of economic development in Latin America submitted to the expert working group, Mexico City, December 12-21, 1961.

Other items that deal with an Orientation to Latin America are:

1103, 1701, 1703, 1708, 2006, 2011, 2014, 2101, 2107, 2110, 2113, 2114, 2117, 2902, 2904, 2909, 2910, 2913, 3102, 3106, 3110, 3112, 3121, 3122, 3125, 3128, 3139, 3140, 3123, 3135, 3144, 3145, 3145, 3147, 3152, 3154, 4002, 4101, 4103, 4107, 4115, 4208, 4902, 5006, 5009, 5014, 5503, 5511, 5566, 5702, 5711, 5722, 5801, 5804, 5812 5814, 5817, 5901, 6010, 6603, 6618

1200. Economic Development

1201. ADELMAN, Irma. Theories of Economic Growth and Development. Stanford: Stanford University Press, 1961.

1202. ALPERT, Paul. Economic Development; Objectives and Methods. New York: Free Press of Glencoe, 1963. 308 pp. Bibliography.

1203. *ASHER, Robert, et al. Development of the Emerging Countries. Washington, D.C.: Brookings Institution, 1962. 239 pp. Bibliographical footnotes.

1204. BAUER, Peter T., and YAMEY, Basil S. The Economics of Under-Developed Countries. Chicago: Chicago University Press, 1957. 271 pp.

1205. ENKE, Stephen. Economics for Development. Englewood Cliffs, New Jersey: Prentice Hall, 1963. 616 pp. Bibliography.

1206. *HIRSCHMAN, Albert O. The Strategy of Economic Development. New Haven: Yale University Press, 1958. 217 pp. Bibliographical footnotes.
A classic in the field.

1207. *HOSELITZ, Berthold F., et al. Theories of Economic Growth. Glencoe, Ill.: Free Press of Glencoe, 1960. 344 pp. Bibliographical references.
Another classic.

1208. LEWIS, William A. Theory of Economic Growth. Homewood, Ill.: Irwin, 1955. 453 pp.

1209. *LIEBENSTEIN, Harry. Economic Backwardness and Economic Growth. New York: John Wiley & Sons, 1960. 295 pp. Bibliographical footnotes.

One of the better books on development.

1210. MILLIKAN, Max F., and BLACKMER, Donald L.M. (eds.). The Emerging Nations. Boston: Little,Brown and Co., 1961. 171 pp. Bibliography.
The book is a result of an MIT seminar.

1211. ROSTOW, Walt W. The Stages of Economic Growth. New York: Cambridge, 1960.
This is the famous and often criticized attempt to classify economic development and put it into stages.

Other items that deal with an Orientation to Economic Development are:

1101, 1102, 1103, 1157, 1702, 1706, 2001, 2008, 2003, 2101, 2112, 2601, 2602, 2603, 2802, 2806, 2906, 2907, 3005, 3007, 3102, 3103, 3104, 3130, 3137, 3139, 3144, 3145, 3156, 3201, 3203, 3402, 4008, 4101, 4103, 4105, 4107, 4208, 4209, 4904, 5005, 5517, 5704, 5709, 5815, 5816, 6013, 6023, 6605, 6614, 6615

1700. Social Change

1701. ADAMS, Richard N., et al. Social Change in Latin America Today. New York: Harper, 1960. 353 pp. Bibliographical footnotes.

The six papers in this volume are contributed by Adams, J. P. Gillin, A. R. Holmberg, O. Lewis, R. W. Patch and C. Wagley with an introduction by Lynan Bryson.

They "indicate that one fundamental fact we now know about Latin America is that all of the countries to the south of us, in varying degrees are undergoing social, economic, and political changes which pain and bewilder their people and make them more difficult to deal with."

1702. ADAMS, Walter, and GARRATY, John A. Is the World Our Campus? East Lansing, Michigan: Michigan State University Press, 1960. 180 pp.

Adams and Garraty point out in blunt terms that all is not well in overseas university projects, that all is not well in AID projects. They give a prescription for change.

1703. FALS-BORDA, Orlando. Peasant Society in the Colombian Andes: A Sociological Study of Saucio. Gainesville: University of Florida Press, 1955. 277 pp. Bibliography.

One of the earlier sociological-anthropological studies of an entire community. Dr. Falls-Borda did the entire study with no institutional sponsorship. He and others have done later studies in the same area. A first rate review of peasant society in Colombia.

1704. HOFFER, Eric. The Ordeal of Change. New York: Harper & Row, 1963. 150 pp.

The San Francisco Longshoreman-philosopher wrote portions of this book in the early 1950's. It is, however, an extremely timely piece. It provides a good companion to W. E. Moore for a reader interested in developing hypotheses in reference to social change.

1705. HUNTER, Floyd. _Community Power Structure: A Study of Decision Makers_. Chapel Hill: University of North Carolina Press, 1953. 297 pp. Bibliography.

Hunter's book,which received mediocre reviews when published twelve years ago, will probably be of great interest to the professional change agent. He has studied only U.S. communities, but his methodological chapter and his conclusions provide considerable food for thought even today.

1706. _Institutional Reforms and Social Development. Trends in Latin America._ Washington, D.C.: Inter-American Development Bank, 1963. 299 pp.

IADB reports here the progress achieved since 1960. It is a chronicle both of specific projects and of measures being taken by each Latin American country.

1707. JELLIFFE, Derrick B., and BENNETT, F. John. "Cultural Problems in Technical Assistance," _Children_, 9 (5):171, September-October, 1962.

Although written by physicians about the problems associated with medical projects, the article has merit for the neophyte who might wonder what he's getting into.

1708. JOHNSON, John J. _The Military and Society in Latin America_. Stanford, California: Stanford University Press, 1964. 308 pp. Bibliography.

The military has played a different role in internal affairs in most Latin American countries from that played by the armed services in the U.S. Professor

Johnson takes us through the nineteenth century and up to today in documenting the military's role. The study "examines the methods available to officers to influence policy decisions . . . . It also treats at length the impact that officers have in the social economic area."

1709. MAIR, Lucy. New Nations. Chicago: University of Chicago Press, 1963. 235 pp. Bibliography.
The study is concerned primarily with the new nations of Africa but both the first chapter, "Nations Remade," and the last, "Social Anthropology and Technological Change," have applicability to any social scientist interested in change.

1710. *MEAD, Margaret (ed.). Cultural Patterns and Technical Change. New York: Mentor, 1955. 352 pp.
Margaret Mead believes that man at last has the technical capacity to advance the well-being of all peoples and that starvation no longer need exist.

1711. MOORE, Wilbert, E. Social Change. (Foundations of Modern Sociology Series.) Englewood Cliffs, New Jersey: Prentice Hall, 1963. 120 pp.
What are the whys and hows of change? Moore tries to think through these questions. (See also Hoffer.)

1712. NAIR, Kusum. Blossoms in the Dust: The Human Factor in Indian Development. Praeger Paperbacks, 1961. 201 pp.
Miss Nair, having traveled throughout India for a year, suggests that attitudes, opinions and beliefs can often be limiting factors in development. As Myrdal says in the introduction: "Her book will contribute to strengthening those who are pleading for a greater emphasis on the human factor in development. Abroad, it will make people realize the true scope of problems and the immense difficulties India has to face."

1713. PIKE, Frederick B. (ed.). The Conflict Between Church and State in Latin America. New York: Alfred A. Knopf, 1964. 240 pp. Bibliography.

Some persons would claim that one cannot understand Latin America without having some feeling for the influence of the Catholic Church.

This is a book of reprints of articles about the place of the church in the fabric of Latin America. The arrangement is historical with the last fifty pages consisting of seven articles on the current scene.

1714. SMITHER, R.R. "Breaking Through the Traditional Village Society: A Theory of Sociological Tactics," Community Development Review, 8 (2):55, June, 1963.

Smither assumes certain factors in the process of change; namely, social groups, mobility of the members and methods of communication. Using these, he then reports the relative success of a project on which he worked.

Other items which deal with an Orientation to Social Change are:

1101, 1102, 1153, 1154, 1156, 2003, 2008, 2010, 2112, 2114, 2117, 2118, 2602, 2806, 2807, 2902, 2908, 2909, 2012, 3013, 3111, 3216, 4002, 4103, 4208, 4902, 5002, 5511, 5512, 5561, 5701, 5706, 5801, 5804, 5805, 5806, 5809, 5810, 5817, 5901, 6013, 6023, 6603, 6608

CHAPTER 2 ECONOMIC DEVELOPMENT

2000 SERIES

2000. Miscellaneous

2001. BAUER, Peter T., and YAMEY, Basil. "Economic Progress and Occupational Distribution," Economic Journal, 61:741, December, 1951.
This is a critical examination and rejection of the Fisher-Clark thesis. The argument is based on factual material on trade in British West Africa. See also a note by the authors, Economic Journal, March, 1954.

2002. DURAN, Eduardo Wiesner. Control Personal De La Economia Colombiana. (Monografia No. 6) Bogota: Centro de Estudios Sobre Desarrollo Economico, Universidad de Los Andes, Julio, 1960.

2003. "Essays in the Quantitative Study of Economic Growth," Economic Development and Cultural Change, 9(3):225-549, April, 1961.
The whole issue is devoted to articles on the above subject.

2004. "Factors of Economic Progress," Social Science Bulletin, 11(2):159-363, 1954.
Most of the entire issue of this quarterly UNESCO publication is devoted to development.

2005. FRANKENHOFF, Charles A. "The Prebisch Thesis: A Theory of Industrialism for Latin America," Journal of Inter-American Studies, 4(2):185-206, April, 1962.

2006. *GALBRAITH, John K. Economic Development. Cambridge: Harvard University Press, 1964. 109 pp.

In this completely revised and much enlarged version of the 1962 book, Economic Development in Perspective, Galbraith stresses the differences in risks for persons who live in rich nations as opposed to those in the poorer ones.

The book should be read in conjunction with T.W. Schultz (1964) and W.W. Rostow (1964).

2007. HAMBRIDGE, Gove. Dynamics of Development, An International Development Reader. New York: Praeger, 1964. 400 pp. Bibliography.

In the foreword,Teadoro Moscoso suggests that the contents of this book provide evidence that international development has come of age. All thirty-two of the articles that make up this book had their genesis in the International Development Review.

2008. HOSELITZ, Berthold F. (ed.). The Progress of Undeveloped Areas. Chicago: University of Chicago Press, 1952. 296 pp.

This book contains lectures given in the summer of 1951. The interest in economic development by social scientists was spurred on by President Truman's fourth point of his inaugural address of January, 1949 (p. 5).

The book,although now thirteen years old, is required reading for the serious student of economic development.

2009. KENADJIAN, B. "Disguised Unemployment in Underdeveloped Countries." Unpublished Ph.D. dissertation, Harvard University, April, 1957.

Originally the term "disguised unemployment" was used by Joan Robinson to describe the adoption of inferior occupations by workers in industrial countries during a depression (1936).

Part I is an excellent review of the theory of disguised unemployment.

Kenadjian suggests that if there is such a thing as disguised unemployment, then improvements in markets would be a help.

Part II discusses disguised unemployment in fact. With the sole exception of a 1928 report on India, he found no factual reports of Asian disguised unemployment.

2010. *MEYNAUD, Jean (ed.). _Social Change and Economic Development_. _Paris: UNESCO, 1963. 210 pp._

Reprints of articles from the _International Social Science Journal_ cover a myriad of subjects of interest to development specialists.

2011. PADDOCK, William, and Paul. _Hungry Nations. Boston: Little, Brown & Co., 1964._ 344 pp. Bibliographical footnotes.

The authors suggest that development must come from within and that achieving it requires much effort.

2012. ROCKEFELLER, Rodman C. "Economic Development and Social Research," _The American Behavioral Scientist_, 8(1):30, September, 1964.

2013. ROGERS, Everett M., and HERZOG, William. "Functional Literacy Among Colombian Peasants," _Economic Development and Cultural Change_. 1965 (in process).

It is widely acknowledged that literacy is a key to national development but there are few reported research efforts on measuring literacy, its consequences, and its antecedents. The main objectives of the present study are: (1) to examine the conceptual nature of literacy; (2) to report the use of a measure of functional literacy; and (3) to determine the correlates of functional literacy among Colombian peasants.

2014. RYCROFT, W. Stanley, and CLEMMER, Myrtle. A Factual Study of Latin America. New York: Office for Research, United Presbyterian Church in the U.S.A., October, 1963. 142 pp. Bibliography.

One of a series of five lithographed handbooks that serve as background studies of the developing areas of the world.

In preface the authors state their purpose: ". . . is to make available some of the constructive thinking being done concerning the development of Latin America . . . . The authors have attempted to describe in broad outline the processes of change in the demographic, political, economic, social, and religious patterns."

2015. SCHULTZ, Theodore. "Investment in Human Capital," The American Economic Review, 51(1):1, March, 1961.

This Presidential address was delivered at the 73rd annual meeting of the American Economic Association. Schultz argues that although the economic value of an education is difficult to determine, the most outstanding feature of the American economic system is the growth of human capital.

2016. VRIES, Egbert de (ed.). Essays on Unbalanced Growth; A Century of Disparity and Convergence. (International Institute of Social Studies, Major Series, Vol. X.) The Hague: Mouton & Co., 1962. 221 pp. Bibliographical references in footnotes.

A most interesting series of essays. The second, "The Distribution of World Income, 1860-1960," is by L. J. Zimmerman, in which he shows, by use of Lorenz curves, that discrepancy between the rich and poor areas of the world has increased in the last 100 years.

Other items that deal with Miscellaneous in a general way include:

1106, 1151, 1152, 1153, 1155, 1157, 1201,
1203, 1204, 1207, 1701, 1703, 1708, 1709, 3005,
3105, 3107, 3111, 3114, 3128, 3130, 3133, 3136,
3142, 3144, 3145, 3201, 3206, 4008, 4010, 4101,
4103, 4209, 5012, 5554, 5561, 5701, 5703, 5709,
5801, 5809, 5810, 5812, 6605, 6609, 6614, 6615,
6818

2100. Area Studies

2101. *ADAMS, Dale, _et al._ _Public Law 480 and Colombia's Economic Development._ Medillin, Colombia: Department of Agricultural Economics, Michigan State University, and Departments De Economia Y Ciencias Socioles Facultad de Agronomia E. Instituto Forestall Universidad Nacional De Colombia, 1964. 384 pp.

A comprehensive study of the country and its agricultural problems creates an excellent book which has several case examples.

2102. BAER, Werner. "Puerto Rico: An Evaluation of a Successful Development Program," _Quarterly Journal of Economics_, 73(4): 645, November, 1959.

Development has stressed external trade. In an interesting analysis of the situation, Mr. Baer sees Puerto Rico's experience as a possible model for other countries which might be linked economically to a large, mature economy.

2103. Committee for Economic Development. _Economic Development of Central America._ Washington: Research and Policy Committee of C.E.D., 1964. 128 pp.

With Spanish and English texts on facing pages. This statement surveys the impact of the Central American Common Market and outlines new steps to be taken to speed economic growth in the area. Includes a history of this common market and a summary of agrarian reform laws.

2104. FURTADO, Celso. _The Economic Growth of Brazil, A Survey from Colonial to Modern Times_. Translated by Ricardo W. de Aquiar and Eric Charles Drysdale. Berkeley: University of California Press, 1963. 285 pp Bibliographical references in footnotes.

Dr. Furtado was formerly chief of the

Development Division of the Economic Commission for Latin America as well as head of the Development Program for the Northeast of Brazil (SUDENE). This is his first work to appear in English and is a translation from Formacao Economica Do Brasil, published in 1959. Furtado claims to present only the outline of development.

The book is an interesting analysis of the story of Brazilian development, although Dr. Furtado claims to present only an outline.

2105. GALBRAITH, John K., and SOLO, Carolyn S. "Puerto Rican Lessons in Economic Development," Annals of the American Academy, 285:55, January, 1953.

The authors note the similarities and differences of Puerto Rico to other developing areas.

2106. FLANDER, M. June. "Prebisch on Protectionism," Economic Journal, 74(294):305, June, 1964.

This paper is an analytical examination of Prebisch's best known statements.

2107. HIRSCHMAN, Albert O. Journeys Toward Progress: Studies of Economic Policy Making in Latin America. New York: Twentieth Century Fund, 1963. 308 pp. Bibliographical footnotes.

Professor Hirschman's latest studies have grown out of some frustrations with the 1961 edition. He studies specific problems and decisions in three countries: Brazil, Chile, and Colombia. In his final chapter, "The Contriving of Reform," he suggests that there is a Latino style. Consequently, he sees the task of the policy-makers as difficult, but filled with opportunities.

2108. Industrial Development of Colombia. A Report to USAID and the Government of Colombia. Prepared by Barrington & Company, Consultants. New York, 1961.

The price control system is cited as a

major reason for inadequate agricultural exploitation and lack of incentive for exports.

2109. U.S. Office of International Trade. Investment in Colombia. Washington, D.C.: U.S. Dept. of Commerce, 1957.
A study of this kind has been done on nearly every nation of the world. Each study provides background on the particular country.

2110. "Latin America," Fortune, 65(2), February, 1962.
Most of the issue is devoted to Latin America. It provides an interesting assessment of many issues, problems and opportunities.

2111. LEWIS, Gordon K, Puerto Rico, Freedom and Power in the Caribbean. New York: Monthly Review Press, 1963. 626 pp. Bibliographical footnotes.

2112. *LIPSKY, G.A., et al. Special Warfare, Area Handbook for Colombia. Prepared by Foreign Areas Studies Division, The American University for Department of the Army, Washington, D.C. : U.S. Government Printing Office, July, 1961.
Although the title may be misleading, this volume is one of the single best sources for orientation which gives sociological, political and economic background to Colombia. The first three sections of the book should be read by those who wish to learn more about Colombia and why it is as it is. The book has no security classification. There are now similar studies for several nations.

2113. MARSHALL-SILVA, J. Inflation and Economic Development. A Case Study: The Chilean Experience 1937-1950. Cambridge: Harvard University Press, 1957.

2114. *POWELSON, John P. Latin America, Today's Economic and Social Revolution. New York: McGraw-Hill, 1964. 303 pp. Bibliographical footnotes.

Dr. Powelson suggests that this book grew out of his association with economics students in Latin America. He wrote the book in order to help establish communications between intellectuals in the United States and Latin America.

Dr. Powelson has also quoted from student papers written for him while he was a visiting professor in Latin America. He has attempted to tackle many of the same burning issues as Peter Nehemkis (Latin America: Myth and Reality). Dr. Powelson frankly discusses, among other things, the issues involved in agrarian reform, business operations and economic planning. (See also Nehemkis)

2115. ROBOCK, Stephen. Brazil's Developing Northeast, A Study of Regional Planning and Foreign Aid. Washington: Brookings Institution, 1963. 213 pp. Bibliographical references.

2116. *STRASSMAN, Wolfgang P. "Is Puerto Rican Economic Development a Special Case?" Inter-American Economic Affairs, 18(1): 61-76, Summer, 1964.

An interesting polemic concerning the Puerto Rican experience.

2117. U.S. House of Representatives. Special Study Mission to Latin America: Peru, Ecuador, Colombia, Panama, Costa Rica. Report No. 223. 88th Cong., 1st Sess., April 23, 1963.

Every country is different, but the problems of transportation are always great and the poor are unhappy.

2118. VERNON, Raymond. The Dilemma of Mexico's Development. Cambridge: Harvard University Press, 1963. 226 pp. Bibliographical references in footnotes.

Vernon gives us an interesting view of the successes and failures of Mexico.

2119. WINTERS, Donald H. Pasos Hacia La Intergracion Centroamericana. Published Master's Thesis, Department of Humanities, Universida Autonoma de San Carlos de Guatemala, 1964, 140 pp. Bibliography.

Other items that deal with Area Studies are:

1105, 1151, 1152, 1153, 1155, 1158, 1201,
1204, 1209, 1210, 1701, 1703, 1706, 1708, 2008,
2010, 2011, 2014, 2015, 2602, 2604, 2605, 2606,
2607, 2808, 3105, 3106, 3107, 3108, 3114, 3121,
3128, 3139, 3214, 3224, 3401, 3410, 3902, 3903,
4010, 4101, 4103, 4104, 4107, 4201, 4202, 4204,
4210, 4904, 5006, 5009, 5509, 5702, 5710, 5712,
5722, 5804, 5809, 5816, 6013, 6614, 6615, 6818

2600. Statistics

2601. Basic Facts and Figures 1961-International Statistics Relating to Education, Culture and Mass Communication. Paris: UNESCO, 1963.
Gives much information on mass media.

2602. Compendium of Social Statistics. 1963. (Statistical Papers Series K, No. 2.) New York: United Nations, 1964.
Statistics, such as they are, for almost every country of the world.

2603. Conceptos, Definiciones Y Metodologia De Las Cuentes Nacionales De Colombia, 1950-1961. Bogota: Banco de La Republica Bogota, 1963.
This paperback booklet gives the background, assumptions, and definitions of National accounts, and would be useful in macro-economic studies of change.

2604. *GINSBURG, Norton S. Atlas of Economic Development. Chicago: University of Chicago Press, 1961. 119 pp. Bibliographical references.
Bert F. Hoselitz, in the foreword, suggests that this book of maps provides the reader with "an analytical tool in the development of a better and more integrated theory of economic growth."
It is a very useful book for the serious student of marketing or development. It also contains a statistical analysis by Brian J. L. Berry.

2605. The Growth of World Industry 1938-1961, National Tables. New York: United Nations, 1963.

2606. KUZNETS, Simon. "Quantitative Aspects of the Economic Growth of Nations: The Share and

Structure and Consumption," Economic Development and Cultural Change, 10(2):Part 2:92, January, 1962.

Three items affect consumption: (1) technology, (2) economic organization, and (3) values guiding the use of income.

2607. Progreso 64/65, Revista del desarrollo latinoamericano. New York: Vision Incorporated, 1964.

The first of what the publishers of Vision plan to be an annual summary of development. The covering letter in this first edition says: "In its pages you will find a most comprehensive analysis of the development and the future economic potential of the Americas."

Interesting and useful articles and statistics.

2608. *Statistical Yearbook, 1963. New York: United Nations, 1964.

Yearbook is similar to the U.S. Statistical Abstract and it is published yearly.

Other items that deal with Statistics are:

1202, 1706, 2001, 2104, 2107, 2801, 2802, 2901, 3005, 3103, 3104, 3105, 3122, 3135, 3214, 3224, 3408, 3410, 4010, 4103, 4211, 4213, 5001, 5503, 5517, 5529, 5712, 5728, 6013, 6602, 6615

2800. Theoretical Issues

2801. BALASSA, Bela A. The Theory of Economic Integration. Homewood, Illinois: Richard D. Irwin, Inc., 1961. 304 pp. Bibliography.

The author discusses static and dynamic effects of nation-state integration and the policy implications of the economic consequences of a fusion of national markets. Chapters 5-7 present growth models, economies of scale, specialization in a large market and external economies in present-day integration projects.

2802. BOULDING, Kenneth E. The Skills of the Economist. Cleveland: Howard Allen, Inc., 1958. 193 pp.

"The economist sees the world not as men and things, but as commodities, and it is precisely in this abstraction that his particular skill resides. A commodity is anything that is scarce . . . . It is not too much to claim that the phenomenon of exchange is at the heart of the economist's abstraction and the ability to recognize and analyze exchange constitutes the core of his skill." Boulding drops such gems throughout the entire book. Views such as Boulding develops add much to the understanding of development.

2803. CLARKSON, Geoffrey P.E. The Theory of Consumer Demand: A Critical Appraisal. Englewood Cliffs, N.J.: Prentice Hall, 1963. 152 pp. Bibliography.

In the preface Clarkson says "This essay is not a treatise on classical theories of consumer behavior. Instead it is an inquiry into the possible existence of an empirically testable theory of consumer demand."

An interesting and original book that should be read by all concerned about better theories of demand.

2804. FRIEDMAN, Milton. A Theory of the Consumption Function. Princeton: Princeton University Press, 1957. 243 pp.

Consumption and income cannot be measured precisely in terms of monthly or annual income. One must break income into permanent and transitory income.

Variability of income is correlated with percent saved, but there is not a word about innovation.

2805. *FURTADO, Celso. Development and Underdevelopment. Translated by Ricardo W. De Aquiar and Eric Charles Drysdale. Berkeley: University of California Press, 1964. 181 pp.

This was translated from a 1961 book Desenvolvemento e Subdesenvolveminto. Dr. Furtado was developing this book over a ten-year period. Parts of the book had appeared in earlier versions as journal articles. He claims that economic theory from the classical, the Keynesian and the Marxian schools all influenced him.

This significant book presents some interesting and original ideas. In the preface, Dr. Furtado says he "is convinced that there is a need for constructive criticism and a reconditioning of economic thought, so that underdevelopment might be more effectively combatted." To contribute to this effort, he presented this book as "a mere groping along in an almost unexplored field" so that new points of departure may be suggested.

2806. HERSKOVITS, Melville J. Economic Anthropology; A Study in Comparative Economics. New York: Alfred A. Knopf, 1952. 547 pp. Bibliography.

A revised and enlarged version of a 1940 book coupled with an extensive review by F. H. Knight and a rebuttal of the review of that earlier book by Mr. Herskovits.

2807. MYINT, Hla. "An Interpretation of Economic Backwardness," Oxford Economic Papers, 6 (2):132, June, 1954.

The author distinguishes between "backward peoples" and "underdeveloped resources." He asks if it is "merely a matter of taste or tact whether we choose to speak of 'backward people' or of 'under-developed human resources.'" He believes the two cannot be superimposed on each other.

The supposition that economic equality and economic development always work in the same direction is a dangerous one. The author believes that "In practice the free play of economic forces in backward countries has resulted, not in a division of labor according to individual abilities, but in a division of labor according to stratified groups." (p. 161)

He argues strongly for countervailing power for the backward people. He believes we can learn three lessons from present and past experience.

1. Some sources of countervailing power, like cooperatives, can be fostered only very slowly.

2. It is easier to redistribute existing incomes than to redistribute and stimulate economic activity by the use of countervailing power.

3. There is a danger of an excessive use of countervailing power combined with extreme nationalism.

2808. SCHUMPETER, Joseph A. The Theory of Economic Development. Cambridge: Harvard University Press, 1934. 255 pp.

The heart of the book is Chapter II, "Fundamentals of Economic Development." The final chapter, "Business Cycles," is relatively outmoded because of government action. It remains a classic.

Other items that deal with Theoretical Issues are:

1153, 1155, 1201, 1202, 1702, 2003, 2005, 2009, 2106, 2603, 2604, 3001, 3003, 3005, 3102, 3106, 3109, 3110, 3111, 3113, 3122, 3130, 3137 3146, 3156, 3202, 3203, 3223, 3401, 3408, 3410, 4010, 4103, 4108, 4201, 4204, 4211, 4212, 4213, 4216, 5001, 5011, 5502, 5503, 5507, 5517, 5529 5561, 5563, 5566, 6013, 6605, 6614, 6615

2900. Bibliographies

2901. DIAZ-BORDENAVE, Juan. "Latin American Research in the Social Sciences." East Lansing: Department of Communications, Michigan State University, 1962. (Mimeographed.)
A bibliography of over 400 articles and books by Latin American researchers.

2902. ________, and LASSEY, William R. "Selected Bibliography on Latin America." East Lansing: Department of Communications, Michigan State University, 1962. (Mimeographed.)
Over 400 articles and books written by Americans.

2903. DURAN, Eduardo Wiesner. Bibliografia Comentada Sobre El Desarrollo Economico Y La Economia Colombiana. Vol. II. Bogota: Centro de Estudios Sobre Desarrollo Economico, Universidad de Los Andes, 1961.
This 714 item annotated bibliography is a treasure for the student of Colombian economic development.

2904. Economic Development and Cultural Change. Chicago: University of Chicago Press.
A quarterly publication. Contains many interesting and useful studies in development.

2905. Informe Anual Del Centro De Investigaciones Sociales 1962-1963. Rio Piedras, Puerto Rico: Centro De Investigaciones Sociales, Universidad de Puerto Rico, 1964. 40 pp.
A complete bibliography of work in progress and completed publications by the staff at the Social Science Research Center. The Center has produced a number of works bearing upon economic development.

2906. International Committee for Social Sciences Documentation. International Bibliography of Economics. Chicago: Aldine Publishing Co.

Published annually in both French and English and is very extensive. A good place to look for works through the eyes of the economist.

2907. International Information Service. Chicago: Library of International Relations.

A quarterly annotated bibliography which "is a guide to documentary sources, scholarly analyses, and significant commentaries on contemporary political, economic and social development in all parts of the world . . . . All materials listed are from the collection of the Library of International Relations and are available . . . on inter-library loan."

This excellent source document was begun in July, 1963, as a reformulation of the periodical, The World in Focus. The first issue of each volume (July) carries an extensive selection of references to current statistical tables, etc.

2908. *KATZ, Sol M., and MCGOWAN, Frank. A Selected List of U.S. Readings on Development. Prepared for the United Nations Conference on the Application of Science and Technology for the Benefit of the less Developed Areas, Agency for International Development. Washington, D.C.: U.S. Government Printing Office, 1963, 363 pp.

This annotated bibliography of 1195 items is a useful addition to the student of development processes. The chapter titles under which the items are grouped are as follows: "The Development Process and Its Setting"; "Planning and Programming"; "Natural Resources"; "Population, Manpower, and Labor Problems"; "Education and Training"; "Health and Sanitation"; "Social Welfare"; "Agriculture"; "Industry"; "Transportation and Trade"; "Communications"; "External Assistance and International Cooperation"; and "Scientific and Technological Policies."

2909. "Lista de Nuevas Adquisiciones." Bogota: Centro de Estudios Sobre Desarrollo Economico, Universidad de Los Andes.

This quarterly mimeographed publication lists by subject areas the acquisitions of one of the best economic libraries in all of Colombia. The library in Bogota would be of great use to persons doing work in the field of Latin American economic development. The Michigan State University library has most of the publications from May, 1960, at the Center in Bogota.

2910. *PARISEAU, Earl J. (ed.). Handbook of Latin American Studies. Gainesville: University of Florida Press.

This book, which is published annually, is a selected annotated bibliography of books, pamphlets and articles on all the various aspects of Latin America. It should be among first works consulted by a researcher interested in this area.

It is broken into subject areas as well as having an author index. Each issue annotates two to five thousand different items.

2911. Report of the Director General on the Activities of the Organization (UNESCO, 1963). Paris: UNESCO, 1964.

A comprehensive report detailing the work of UNESCO in 1963. It tells of work completed and underway. UNESCO is a valuable information source for anyone doing social science research in developing nations.

2912. RYCROFT, W. Stanley, and CLEMMER, Myrtle M. "Bibliography for Latin American Studies." Office for Research, The United Presbyterian Church in the U.S.A., December, 1963. (Mimeographed.)

This bibliography was compiled during the preparation of A Factual Study in Latin America. The price is thirty-five cents for this eighteen-page helper. Excellent and comprehensive bibliography.

2913. Special Collection of Books, for the Seventh World Conference of The Society For International Development. Alexandria, Va. :The Conference Book Service Inc., 1965. 10 pp. (Lithographed.)

A list of 233 recently published books concerning the area of development. The lists of forty-three publishers were gleaned for this listing. The pamphlet was distributed free of charge at the conference.

2914. SPENCER, Dao N. (ed.). U.S. Non-Profit Organizations. Voluntary Agencies, Missions and Foundations participating in Technical Assistance Abroad, A Directory, 1964. New York: Technical Assistance Information Clearing House, 1964.

TAICH is the clearing house arm of the American Council of Voluntary Agencies for Foreign Service Inc. under a contract with U.S. Agency for International Development. In late 1963 questionnaires were mailed to over four hundred organizations. This edition of the directory contains profiles of almost two hundred and fifty organizations. The first part of the directory lists organization profiles while the second part lists country by country the various programs now under way.

2915. WASSON, Donald (ed.). American Agencies Interested in International Affairs. New York: Frederick A. Praeger, 1964. 200 pp.

This fifth edition attempts to describe private organizations which conduct programs of research in international affairs or which conduct or sponsor meetings and information programs on a continuing basis. Two hundred and ninety-three different organizations are listed. There are both subject and personnel indexes. The information on the organizations includes such items as head personnel, purposes, organization and publications or activities.

2916. World Agricultural Economic and Rural Sociology Abstracts Journal. Amsterdam: North Holland Publishing Company.
Published quarterly since 1959. Each issue contains about 200 pages.

Other items that deal with Bibliographies are:

1105, 1151, 1201, 1203, 1706, 2107, 2808, 3111, 4103

In addition, note the other bibliographical sections.

CHAPTER 3 MARKETING

3000 SERIES

3000. Miscellaneous

3001. BARGER, Harold. Distribution's Place in the American Economy Since 1869. Princeton: Princeton University Press, 1955. 222 pp. Bibliographical footnotes.

A standard reference on measures of productivity in the distributive sector in the U.S. since 1869.

3002. BAUER, Peter T., and YAMEY, Basil. "The Economics of Marketing Reform," Journal of Political Economy, 62(3):210, June, 1954.

This paper discusses the impact and implications of ". . . a miscellany of measures designed to improve agricultural marketing . . . . These include reduction in the number of intermediaries, control of the channels of marketing, delimitation of the places where transactions may take place, elimination of inferior grades of products, and so forth."

3003. DEMSETZ, Harold. "The Effect of Consumer Experience on Brand Loyalty and the Structure of Market Demand," Econometrica, 30 (1):22, January, 1962.

The purpose of the paper is to both quantify and test for changes in the success of manufacturers' efforts to differentiate their products as consumers gain more experience with them. The test case considered here lends support to the position that consumers do learn from experience.

3004. DRUCKER, Peter F. Managing for Results. New York: Harper & Row, 1964. 240 pp. Bibliography.

Drucker states the following generalizations about businesses in the first chapter. The remainder of the book consists of elaboration of these ideas.

1. Neither results nor resources exist inside the business. Both exist outside.
2. Results are obtained by exploiting opportunities, not by solving problems.
3. Resources to produce results must be allocated to opportunities rather than to problems.
4. Economic results are earned only by leadership.
5. Any leadership position is transitory and likely to be short-lived.
6. What exists is getting old.
7. What exists is likely to be misallocated.
8. Concentration is the key to economic results.

3005. HAMILTON, Earl J. "Prices as a Factor in Business Growth," The Journal of Economic History, 12(4):325, Fall, 1952.

Hamilton suggests that the price mechanism has worked well. He doubts that economic planners for underdeveloped areas can hit upon a more effective device for either restraining consumption or inducing investment than rising prices and lagging wages. He says "It has not been unusual in war or peace for an individual or group to make sacrifices for others, including future generations; and the sacrifices of real income and leisure by workers that I have singled out as dynamic factors in economic development, though spread over long periods, developed too slowly to be crushing on any. Think of the rich rewards in income and leisure they have borne succeeding generations." An interesting thesis has been presented.

3006. *HOLTON, Richard. "Changing Demand and Consumption," in Labor Commitment and Social Change in Developing Areas. Wilbert Moore and Arnold Feldman (eds.). New York: Social Science Research Council, 1960. p. 201.

The author discusses how the consumption expenditure pattern will affect the whole fabric of economic growth. There is special reference to how urbanization and imitative consumption generate demand for imported goods and act as constraint on the growth of the indigenous manufacturing sector.

3007. HOSELITZ, Berthod F. "The Market Matrix," in Labor Commitment and Social Change in Developing Areas. Wilbert Moore and Arnold Feldman (eds.). New York: Social Science Research Council, 1960. p. 217.

The author discusses nonintersecting exchange systems, the two faces of a market and the market as a mechanism of growth.

3008. KATONA, George. The Mass Consumption Society. New York: McGraw Hill, 1964. 343 pp. Bibliography.

3009. MCLELLAND, W.G. "Economics of the Supermarket," The Economic Journal, 72(285): 154, March, 1962.

Although the article is descriptive regarding supermarkets in Britain, the author has also listed prerequisites for supermarket development. He outlines the conditions as follows: freedom to build; certain conditions of supply; and freedom to price competitively.

3010. MINTZ, Sidney W. "Market Systems and Whole Societies," Economic Development and Cultural Change, 12(4):444, July, 1964.

3011. OXENFELDT, Alfred R. (ed.). Models of Markets. New York: Columbia University Press, 1963. 371 pp. Bibliographical references in footnotes.

Oxenfeldt has collected an interesting group of papers. Two examples from these papers are below.

Richard Heflebower suggests that theory is devoid of empirical content; it merely specifies the empirical evidence that is relevant and the functional relationship among variables.

Boulding tells us that when a body of theory cannot account for an important social phenomenon and, in addition, when it seems to involve assumptions which clearly violate the mass of social reality, it is obviously slated for some drastic revision.

3012. TAX, Sol. "Changing Consumption in Indian Guatemala," Practical Anthropology, 9(1): 15-26, January-February, 1962.

3013. WHARTON, Clifton, Jr. "Aiding the Community: A New Philosophy for Foreign Operations," Harvard Business Review, 32(2):64, March-April, 1954.

Companies operating in foreign areas must reckon with the mood of the times. Wharton argues persuasively that in its own self-interest management needs be concerned about the communities within which it operates.

3014. ________. "Marketing, Merchandising and Moneylending: A Note on Middleman Monopsony in Malaya," Malayan Economic Review, 7:24, October, 1962.

A theoretical analysis of the necessary and sufficient conditions for existence of monopsony and oligopsony in a low income rural area.

Other items that deal with Marketing are:

2108, 4002, 4004, 4010, 4103, 4108, 4115, 4209, 4212, 4216, 4901, 5515, 5551, 5559, 5709, 5814, 5815, 6001, 6021, 6605, 6613, 6813

3100. Area Studies

3101. Adjuste de instalaciones y practicas de comercializacion de granos en Argentina de acuerdo a las necesidades que se proyectan. Buenos Aires: Consejo Nacional de Desarrollo, 1962.

3102. ARMKNECHT, Richard F., Jr. "Marketing in Puerto Rico: Industrial Distribution in a Developing Economy," Proceedings of the American Marketing Association, p. 444, Winter, 1961.

In a short speech Mr. Armknecht argues for more attention to industrial distribution. He pleads for government help in distribution as a part of the Commonwealth's program of development.

3103. BALCAZAR, J., ALVARO, and KYLE, L. "Costo de Produccion de Leche en el Departament del Valle." Faculted de Agronomia de Palmira Universidad Nacional, Cali, Colombia, April, 1959.

A factual study of costs of milk production in a specific area of Colombia.

3104. BARTELS, Robert (ed.). Comparative Marketing: Wholesaling in Fifteen Countries. Homewood, Illinois: Irwin, 1963. 317 pp. Bibliography.

Dr. Bartel's collection contains mostly descriptive studies of wholesaling practices. His interesting concluding chapter cites the need for more comparative studies.

3105. BOHANNAN, Paul, and DALTON, George (eds.). Markets in Africa. Evanston: Northwestern University Press, 1963. 762 pp. Bibliography.

This book contains twenty-seven papers on various historical and contemporary aspects of economic development in Africa presented by anthropologists, economists and sociologists at a conference sponsored by Social Science Research Council at Northwestern University in 1961. See especially the extended treatment of markets in primitive economies compared with developed economies which was written by Bohannan (anthropologist) and Dalton (economist).

3106. BOYD, Harper W., Jr., CLEWETT, Richard M., and WESTFALL, Ralph L. "The Marketing Structure of Venezuela," Journal of Marketing, 22(4):391, April, 1958.

The article describes the actions of consumers, retailers, and wholesalers in Venezuela with major emphasis on the lack of price competition prevalent in the market.

3107. BRANSON, R.E. "The Structure and Efficiency of Food Marketing in Puerto Rico." Unpublished Ph.D. dissertation, Harvard University, 1954

Food shortages in and following World War II led SSRC of Univ. of Puerto Rico to request an extensive study of food marketing. Harvard agreed to sponsor. Branson gathered his information in 1950-51.

3108. CANAS-L., Washington. "Food Retailing Practices in Chile," Journal of Retailing, 37 (3):32, Fall, 1961.

The article describes conditions, but it is not of much value.

3109. CHRISTIAN, Richard C. "Challenges of Global Marketing," Journal of Marketing, 25(4): 72, April, 1962.

The author discusses some of the opportunities involved in distribution in other countries. In addition, he also gives operational suggestions for improving marketing.

3110. COOK, Hugh L. "Some Structural Characteristics of the Venezuelan Milk Industry," _Journal of Farm Economics_, 47(1):132, February, 1965.

A descriptive study of the milk industry in Venezuela. Cook suggests that changes in government policy may be needed to maintain the viability of the industry.

3111. DALTON, George. "Traditional Production in Primitive African Economies," _Quarterly Journal of Economics_, 76(3):360, August, 1962.

Dalton discusses the role played by the three exchange systems--reciprocity, redistribution and market--in contemporary African economics and how these differ from Western economy because of the absence of market exchange.

3112. _Development of Agricultural Marketing and Cooperatives in Latin America and the Caribbean_. Washington, D.C.: International Cooperation Administration, 1959.

Report of a seminar held in Kingston, Jamaica, November, 1959. Discussion of problems throughout marketing. There are summary statements for most every Latin country.

3113. *DEWEY, Alice G. _Peasant Marketing in Java_. New York: Free Press of Glencoe, 1962. 238 pp. Bibliography.

The three purposes of this research project were (1) to link the market system with the larger economic and social structure of the society, (2) to show that underdeveloped societies are composed of interdependent units, and (3) to examine the techniques Javanese traders use to compete with different groups.

Benjamin Higgins reviewed this book unfavorably and criticized Miss Dewey's use of economic analysis. Higgins does point out, though, that one of the main lessons of the Dewey book, to which he subscribes, is that economists ought not worry too much about assumed differences in economic behavior between one society and another, particularly between advanced and underdeveloped countries. See the review of Peasant Marketing in Java in The American Journal of Sociology, Vol. LXVII (Nov., 1962), 383-384.

3114. DUNBAUGH, Frank M. Marketing in Latin America. New York: Printer's Ink Book Company, 1960. 298 pp. Bibliography.

The object of the book is twofold. First, it delineates present-day Latin America as a market for goods and services. Second, it gives executives and students of business administration an insight into the actual workings of the marketing of goods and services in Latin America.

3115. EWING, John S. "Discount Houses in Australia and Mexico," Journal of Marketing, 26(3):37, July, 1962.

Consultants advised against it, but an entrepreneur established discount houses in Mexico. They have been successful.

3116. FLORENS, A.A. "Algunos Aspectos del Mercadeo de Carne de Pollo en Puerto Rico." (Bulletin of Puerto Rico Agricultural Experiment Station, No. 152.) English summary. July, 1960.

3117. ____________. "Experiencias en la Venta de Pinas en Supermercados." (Bulletin of Puerto Rico

Agricultural Experiment Station, E. & S.R. 58.) English summary. Feb., 1960.

3118. ________, and PEDRAZA-G., R. "Marketing of Pineapples in Puerto Rico." (Bulletin of Puerto Rico Agricultural Experiment Station, E. & S.R. 175.) English summary. Dec., 1963.

3119. FOSTER, George M. "The Folk Economy of Rural Mexico with Special Reference to Marketing," Journal of Marketing, 13(2): 153, October, 1948.

3120. *FOSTER, Phillips W. "Some Domestic Agricultural Marketing Problems of Colombia." Unpublished Ph.D. dissertation, University of Illinois, 1958.

Even though Mr. Foster concentrates mainly on egg marketing for his examples, this text is one of the first definitive studies of marketing in an urban area of Colombia.

3121. FRANCO-COMACHO, G. Mercado de la Papa Respecto a Bogota D.E. (CEDE Monografia No. 2.) Bogota: Universidad de Los Andes, 1959.

3122. *GALBRAITH, John K., and HOLTON, Richard H. Marketing Efficiency in Puerto Rico. Cambridge, Mass.: Harvard University Press, 1954. 204 pp.

This is the bible for the study of marketing of consumer non-durables in Puerto Rico. One shortcoming for the reader wishing to duplicate this study is the paucity of procedural data.

3123. GARCIA-O., R., and PRINGLE, G.E. "Costs and Efficiency of Retail Milk Routes in the San Juan Metropolitan Area." (Bulletin of Puerto Rico Agricultural Experiment Station, E. & S.R. 174.) English summary. Dec., 1963.

3124. GEIGER, Theodore. The General Electric Company in Brazil, Ninth Case Study in an NPA Series of U.S. Business Performance Abroad. Washington, D.C.: National Planning Association, January, 1961. 106 pp.
Another of the case studies. See also R. Woods (Item 3156) and S. May (Item 3138) for other publications in this series.

3125. HARRISON, T., FLEMING, N. and MARSHALL, H. "Report on Consulting Assignment Conducted November 15 through November 28, 1956,with the Office of Food Distribution of the Economic Development Administration (Puerto Rico)." 1956. (Mimeographed.) 12 pp.
This is a follow-up to the Galbraith and Holton report.

3126. HADDOCK, D., and MARABAL, R.A. "Preferencias del Consumidar par la Batata." (Bulletin of Puerto Rico Agricultural Experiment Station, E. & S.R. 110.) English summary. May, 1963.

3127. HAWKINS, H.C.G. Wholesale and Retail Trade in Tanganyika. New York: Praeger, 1965. 160 pp.
This is a pioneering study of market structure in Tanganyika. The book offers insight into the trade potential of other East African areas. It is another of the Praeger Studies in International Economics and Development.

3128. HERNANDEZ-G., Jose M. "Cooperatives Agricolas y pecuarias de Colombia sus perspectives de exito en produccion y mercadeo." (CEDE Monografia No. 13.) Bogota: Universidad de Los Andes, 1962. (Mimeographed.) 113 pp.

3129. HERNANDEZ-P., E. "The Application of Modern Marketing Techniques in Latin America," Mexican American Review, 27(6):14, June, 1959.
The text of a speech given before the International Chamber of Commerce in Washington, April 21, 1959, is presented

in this article. The author, who is a Mexican business executive, suggests that ". . . . The main marketing fact about Latin America today is that it is an exploding market." Using a definition of marketing similar to McCarthy's, the author feels Latin American marketing men have hardly begun to meet the needs of the market and should concentrate on the mass market.

3130. HOLTON, Richard H. "Economic Development and the Growth of the Trade Sector in Italy," Banca Nazionale del Lavoro: Quarterly Review, 62:240, September, 1962.
Mr. Holton discusses the role of retail trade in the process of economic development in Italy over the 1951-61 period. He concludes that it cannot be proved or disproved that there is excess capacity in retailing in Italy, that the proportion of the work force in retail trade can be expected to increase even if excess capacity is gradually eliminated, and that entry restrictions on large-scale retailing should be removed. (Moreover, he seeks to correct the popular conception of the changes in U.S. retailing which exaggerates the strength of the large retail stores and firms.)

3131. JOHNSON, S.E., et. al. Report on India's Food Crisis and Steps to Meet it. Ford Foundation and Government of India, April, 1959.
The authors suggest establishment of quality standards, uniform weights and measures, as well as dissemination of reliable and timely market information.

3132. KAPLAN, S. "Food for a City: Mexico's Supermarkets on Wheels," Americas, 14:34, May, 1962.

3133. KATZIN, Margaret. "The Business of Higglering in Jamaica," Social and Economic Studies, Kingston, Jamaica, 9(3):297,

September, 1960.
The author analyzed weekly operating statements extending over more than one year to examine the economic efficiency of the intermediaries through which food grown on small farms is brought to consumers.

3134. KELLER, H.R. Some Observations and Recommendations on Wool Marketing in Chile. Chile: USAID Research Report.
A contractor surveyed the entire wool industry in Chile. The study covered the production, shearing,marketing, and milling of Chilean wools in every province from Coquimbo in the north to Magallanes at the southernmost tip.

3135. KEYES, S., ZAPATA-A., J., AND HADDOCK, D. "Mercado Potencial Para Los Productos Agricoles de Puerto Rico Compras Que Hacen Hoteles y Restaurentes." (Bulletin of Puerto Rico Agricultural Experiment Station, E. & S.R. 150.) Sept., 1959.

3136. LOCKLEY, Lawrence C. A Guide to Market Data in Central America. Tegucigalpa, Hondures: Central American Bank for Economic Integration, 1964. 162 pp. Bibliography.
This guide brings together the available marketing information for the five Common Market countries of Central America. The author believes this to be a pioneering effort for Central America. The guide covers population, purchasing power, pre-disposition to buy, susceptibility to sales promotional efforts, wholesale establishments, and retailing. It can be purchased at U.S. $2.00 per copy plus U.S. $0.80 for postage from the publisher.

3137. MARTIN, L.R. "Some Marketing Problems in Pakistan and India," Journal of Farm Economics, 41:1323, December, 1959.

The author comments on three characteristics of underdeveloped nations (lack of marketing facilities, unreliable market channels, and underemployed labor) that make the application of economic efficiency concepts inappropriate in underdeveloped areas.

3138. MAY, S. and PLAZA, G. United States Business Performance Abroad, The Case Study of the United Fruit Company in Latin America. Washington: National Planning Association, 1958.

A comprehensive report of the contribution of United Fruit to the host countries and to the United Fruit stockholders.

3139. MINTZ, Sidney W., and HALL, Douglas. "The Origins of the Jamaican Internal Marketing System," Yale University Publications in Anthropology, No. 57, 1960.

A historical analysis of the involvement of internal food through the mid-nineteenth century.

3140. MINTZ, Sidney W. "Role of the Middleman in the Internal Distribution System of a Caribbean Peasant Economy," Human Organization, 15(2):18-23, Summer, 1956.

As noted in MIT Bibliography, 1964.

This article is related to the preceding one in that the observations for both were made in Jamaica. This one deals with the central role of middlemen in distributing food and thereby supplying the cash nexus between producer and consumer.

3141. OLIVIERI-R., J.A. "Market Organization Patterns and Related Problems in Latin America." Unpublished Ph.D. dissertation, University of Wisconsin, 1961. (University Microfilms No. 61-5957.)

A look at marketing in Latin America by a Puerto Rican. The thesis topic is broad, so that it serves only as an introduction.

3142. PEDROZA-G., R., RODRIGUEZ-V., S., and QUINTERO-A., J.L. "Production and Marketing of Oranges in Puerto Rico: The Middlemen." 1956-57. (Bulletin of Puerto Rico Agricultural Experiment Station, E. & S.R. 62.) July, 1960.

3143. PRINGLE, G.E., VELEZ-O., R., and MARIANO-R., J. "Costas de Recollecion de Leche Cruda en Puerto Rico." (Bulletin of Puerto Rico Agricultural Experiment Station, E. & S.R. 50.) January, 1960.

3144. PRINGLE, G.E. "A Study of Fluid Milk Marketing Costs and Prices in Puerto Rico." (Bulletin of Puerto Rico Agricultural Experiment Station, E. & S.R. 158.) May, 1961.

3145. RODRIGUEZ-G., O., and CANDELLAS, J.B. "Agricultural Statistics of Puerto Rico, 1935-59." (Bulletin of Puerto Rico Agricultural Experiment Station, E. & S.R. 60.) June, 1960.

3146. RANDHAWA, N.S., and HEADY, E.O. "Decision-Making Under Uncertainty with Special Reference to Agriculture (in India)," Indian Journal of Agricultural Economics, 18(3):9, July, 1963.

Decision-making can involve three uncertainties: technological, innovation, and price. The main emphasis of paper is on technological uncertainty.

3147. SHAW, R.L. "Incaparina Market Testing Program in Colombia." Prepared for the Institute of Nutrition of Central America and Panama, 1963. (Mimeographed.)

INCAPARINA is the high-protein, low-cost food supplement developed by the Instituto de Nutricion de Centre America y Panama. INCAPARINA was introduced into Cali,

Colombia, by Productos Quaker S.A. The introduction was successful.

3148. SAYRES, William C. "Indians and the Market: Model and Mode in a Colombian Community," The American Journal of Economics and Sociology, 16(1):1, October, 1956.
According to the local lore, Indians of the Popayan area of Columbia are shrewd bargainers. This is the belief of the Indians themselves as well as the local shopkeepers. Sayres' investigations indicated that contrary to the popular belief, the Indians were usually poor bargainers.

3149. SRIVASTAVA, R.S. Agricultural Marketing in India and Abroad. Bombay, India: Vora and Co., 1960. 243 pp. Bibliography.
The book is a rewrite of a thesis embodying research done in 1946-48. Thus many of the figures are outdated. The layout and the methodology are interesting. The author believes the inefficiencies call for more government control.

3150. "Status of Marketing in Underdeveloped Countries," L'Egypte Contemporaine, 49(294): 37-43, October, 1958.

3151. *STALEY, Charles E. "A Case Study of Response to Agricultural Prices in Costa Rica," Economic Journal, 71(282):432, June, 1961.
In 1955-56 the prices of beans, rice and corn were changed. The paper attempts to measure the response of production.

3152. TAYLOR, Donald A. "Retailing in Brazil," Journal of Marketing, 24(1):54, July, 1959.
Mr. Taylor discusses types of retail establishments in Brazil and changes in retail sales.

3153. UNDERWOOD, F.W. "The Marketing System in Peasant Haiti," Yale University Publications in Anthropology, No. 60, 1960.

The field notes and published sources making up this interesting report all date back to the 1940's. Still, it is useful for the depth of the report.

3154. VARGAS-HERNANDEZ,D., FLORENS, A.A., and MALDONADO, J.L. "Marketing Structure of Poultry Meat in Puerto Rico, 1959-60." (Bulletin of Puerto Rico Agricultural Experiment Station, No. 169.) August, 1963.

3155. WEBB, K.E. "Problems of Food Supply in Brazil," Journal of Inter-American Studies, 3:239, April, 1961.

3156. WOOD, Richardson, and KEYSER, Virginia. Sears, Roebuck de Mexico, S.A. Washington: National Planning Association, 1953. 67 pp.

This is the first of a series on United States business performance abroad. In undertaking these studies, the National Planning Association said, "We are attempting only to sketch out those aspects of typical managerial efforts that contribute to the general economic and social progress of a host country."

Many contend that in an undeveloped economy, the contribution of a distributive organization is of little importance compared to those that generate savings and investment. However, the Sears story in Mexico offers some serious arguments against this viewpoint.

3157. ZAPATA-A.,J., and HADDOCK, D. "Mercado Potencial Para los Productos Agricoles de Puerto Rico--Compras del Gobierno del Estado Libre Asociado de Puerto Rico." (Bulletin of Puerto Rico Agricultural Experiment Station, No. 154.) English summary. July, 1960.

3158. ______________. "Potential Market for Agricultural Products of Puerto Rico--Exports to the U.S. and Foreign Countries." (Bulletin of Puerto Rico Agricultural Experiment Station, No. 171.) September, 1961.

3159. ZAPATA, L.R. De, ZAPATA-A., J., and HADDOCK, D. "Potential Market for Agricultural Products of Puerto Rico--Purchases Made By Food Processing Plants." (Bulletin of Puerto Rico Agricultural Experiment Station, No. 167. July, 1963.

Other items which deal with Area Studies (3100 Series) are:

1105, 2001, 2011, 2015, 2108, 2109, 2110, 2116, 2602, 2604, 2606, 2607, 3008, 3010, 3011, 3201, 3202, 3206, 3404, 3901, 4010, 4103, 4105, 4107, 4108, 4115, 4210, 4214, 5004, 5009, 5527, 5528, 5722, 5813, 5814, 6013, 6014, 6021, 6605

3200. Economic Development

3201. ABBOTT, John C. "Marketing and Area Development Studies," Proceedings of the American Marketing Association, p. 424, December, 1963.

3202. *BONNEN, John T., EICHER, Carl K., and SCHMID, A.J. "Marketing in Economic Development," Chapter 3 from Agricultural Market Analysis. Vern Sorenson (ed.). East Lansing: Michigan State University, 1964. pp.35-68.

An examination of the role of marketing in economic development in advanced and in underdeveloped nations.

3203. BURNET, I.D. "Stimulating Development Through Consumption Oriented Policies," International Development Review, 6(3):21, September, 1964.

It is the argument of this paper that an appreciation of the consumption patterns of a developing area and incentives to make the most of existing productive capacity are sometimes more important than an extension of productive capacity.

3204. CHATURVEDI, J.N. Theory of Marketing in Underdeveloped Countries. Allahabad, India: Kitab Mahal Publishers, 1959. 135 pp.

The author suggests that a theory of real and forced marketable surplus is more applicable to underdeveloped economies than the real marketable surplus approach used in developed nations. He develops the forced market theory and explains the reasons it is characteristic of underdeveloped areas.

3205. *COLLINS, N.R., and HOLTON, Richard H. "Programming Changes in Marketing in Planned Economic Development," Kyklos, 16:123, January, 1963. Reprinted in Agriculture in Economic Development, C. Eicher and L. Witt, (eds.). New York: McGraw-Hill, 1964.

The authors suggest that changes in the organization of the marketing system may be necessary if changes in production are to be realized in an underdeveloped area. Further, they suggest that marketing might act as a leading factor to encourage changes in the productive sector. Special reference is made to southern Italy as one example of a situation where this theory could apply.

3206. COPULSKY, William. "Forecasting Sales in Underdeveloped Countries," _Journal of Marketing_, 24(1):36, July, 1959.

Marketing has been neglected in developing countries. The use of marketing research techniques can reduce differences between productive capacity and demand.

3207. *FIRTH, Raymond, and YAMEY, Basil S., (eds.). _Capital Saving and Credit in Peasant Societies_. Chicago: Aldine, 1964. 393 pp.

This book is a major effort by anthropologists to present their observations of the economic systems in communities they have closely studied.

3208. HIRSCH, Leon V. _Marketing in an Underdeveloped Economy: The North Indian Sugar Industry_. Englewood Cliffs, New Jersey: Prentice-Hall, 1961. 392 pp. Bibliographical footnotes.

A case study. It is one of the winning Ford Foundation Ph.D. dissertations.

3209. *HOLLANDER, Stanley C. "Retailing: Cause or Effect," _Proceedings of the American Marketing Association_, p. 220, December, 1962.

Dr. Hollander's extensive knowledge of the field of retailing and the great number of footnotes makes the article very useful.

Hollander suggests "our recorded retail history does seem to reveal some fairly clearcut connections between environment and the kinds of retailing that will be fostered."

3210. HOLTON, Richard H. "Food Retailing and Economic Growth," Journal of Farm Economics, 38:356-60, May, 1960.

3211. ________. "Marketing Structure and Economic Development," Quarterly Journal of Economics, 67(3):344, August, 1953.

3212. ________. "Price Discrimination at Retail: The Supermarket Case," Journal of Industrial Economics, 6(1):28, October, 1957.

3213. *HOSELITZ, Berthold F., and MOORE, Wilbert E. (eds.). Industrialization and Society. Paris: UNESCO, 1963.

This is the report of another conference sponsored by UNESCO. Moore suggests on page 364 that "the conference demonstrated the utility - and indeed the necessity - of an interdisciplinary approach to the complex phenomena of economic development . . . . For many purposes interdisciplinary research teams are essential . . . however, there is also growing need for 'inter-disciplinary individuals' . . ."

3214. *HOYT, Elizabeth E. "The Impact of a Money Economy on Consumption Patterns," Annals of the American Academy, 305:12, May, 1956.

The author's subject is the effect on consumption patterns of situations in which new money income results from new opportunities to make or earn money under conditions of technological change.

She suggests that "we have no complete picture of the impact of economic change on consumption patterns in even one underdeveloped society. Economic change has been studied much more frequently from an interest in production or interest in distribution than from an interest in consumption."

3215. KINDLEBERGER, Charles P. Economic Development. New York: McGraw-Hill Book Company, Inc., 1958. 325 pp.

In Chapter six the author discusses specifically the following topics related to the market and market organization: The size of the market, growth of markets, markets and money, and distribution and development.

3216. *"Marketing - Its Role in Increasing Productivity," (Freedom From Hunger Campaign Basic Study No. 4.) Rome: Food and Agriculture Organization, 1962.

"The marketing of agricultural products is vitally important in any campaign to free the world from hunger for two main reasons. Most of those who go hungry do so because the food they need costs more than they can afford. Since a large part of the price is often made up of marketing costs, it is clear that high marketing costs are an important reason why some people have not enough food . . . . The second main reason for stressing the significance of marketing is its impact on production." Marketing can provide adequate incentives for increasing production.

3217. MEHREN, George L. "Market Organization and Economic Development," Journal of Farm Economics, 41(4):1307, December, 1959.

This article considers seven general questions about marketing in underdeveloped areas. It contains a list of hypotheses that may suggest answers to why the traditional market structure exists.

3218. ________. "Market Structure and Market Procedures in Economic Development," Malayan Economic Review, 4(1):94, April, 1959.

The hypothesis presented is that market structure in all countries is in a sort of balance with other segments of the food industries. Thus changes in any segment--marketing or others--induced by government are unlikely to be successful unless consistent changes are made in all segments."

3219. MYERS, Kenneth H. "Marketing's Role in the Economy," Proceedings of the American Marketing Association, p. 355, Dec., 1963.
Myers asks, what is the role of marketing in economic development of the U.S. as shown by history, and what are the implications? He believes that industry is adaptive to society and the marketing department is adaptive to strategy of firm.

3220. NIEUWENHUIJZE, Christoffel A.O. van. Markets and Marketing as Factors of Development in the Mediterranean Basin (Mediterranean Social Science Research Council). The Hague: Mouton & Co., 1963.

3221. POLANYI, Karl, ARENSBERG, Conrad M., and PEARSON, Harry W. (eds.). Trade & Market in the Early Empires. Glencoe, Illinois: Free Press, 1957. 382 pp.
This book is the product of a joint effort by economists and anthropologists. The authors argue that historical evidence indicates that only a small number of alternative patterns of organizing man's livelihood exist. Conveniently, their methodology is not limited only to the money sector of an economy. The methodology is built around such questions as: "Who did what to whom? In what order? How often? Where?"

3222. *ROSTOW, Walt W. The View from the Seventh Floor. New York: Harper & Row, 1964. 178 pp.
The book is based upon speeches and articles that Rostow has made since taking office as Chairman of the Policy Planning Council of the U.S. Department of State.
Chapter 10, "The Nationalization of Takeoff," and 11, "How to Make a National Market," are of special interest to the

student of development with an eye to marketing.

3223. SHAPIRO, Stanley J. "Comparative Marketing and Economic Development," in Science in Marketing. George Schwartz (ed.). New York: John Wiley and Sons, Inc., 1965. pp. 398-429 (chapter 14).
Mr. Shapiro presents what he considers to be the seven main issues concerning the role of marketing in economic development. He does so in a frank and interesting manner.

3224. WELLS, O.V. "Market Structure for Economic Development," in Proceedings of the International Conference of Agricultural Economists. London: Oxford University Press, p. 131, 1963.

Other items that deal with Economic Development are:

2104, 2108, 2110, 2116, 2117, 2801, 2808,
3005, 3404, 3405, 3406, 3407, 4008, 4009, 4101,
4103, 4107, 4202, 4203, 4204, 5004, 5527, 5551,
5709, 5722, 5728, 6003, 6013, 6014, 6614, 6615

In addition, most all series 3100 items apply to this section.

3400. Food and Agriculture

3401. ABBOTT, John C. "Food Marketing in Western Europe Today," Journal of Marketing, 27 (2):17, April, 1963.
This is one of several articles about marketing in a particular country or area that has appeared recently in the Journal of Marketing. These articles can be of use for a general orientation.

3402. ________. Marketing Eggs and Poultry. (Marketing Guide No.4.) Rome: Food and Agriculture Organization, 1961.
A "how to do it" book for persons wishing to establish businesses in developing nations.

3403. ________. Marketing Fruits and Vegetables. (Marketing Guide No. 2.) Rome: Food and Agriculture Organization, 1958.

3404. ________. Marketing Livestock & Meat. (Marketing Guide No. 3.) Rome: Food and Agriculture Organization, 1960.

3405. ________. Marketing Problems and Improvement Programs. (Marketing Guide No. 1.) Rome:Food and Agriculture Organization, 1958.
Abbott outlines the importance of marketing (which he defines as all activities except processing) which take place on farm products between the farm and the place of ultimate consumption.

3406. ________. "The Role of Marketing in the Growth of Agricultural Production and Trade in Less Developed Countries," Food and Agriculture Organization, Monthly Bulletin of Agricultural Economics and Statistics. Vol. 9(9): 1, September, 1960.

3407. BILLON, F. "Orientacion Neuva de Una Politica a Nacional de Mercadeo de la Carne." Report of National Planning Association of Colombia. May 10, 1963. (Typewritten.)

An evaluation of meat distribution in Bogota and a plan for improving it. Dr. Billon is a researcher with the Colombian National Planning Association.

3408. DIGBY, M., and GRETTON, R.H. Cooperative Marketing for Agricultural Producers. (Agricultural Development Paper 53.) Rome: Food and Agriculture Organization, 1957.
Principles of marketing and a "how to do it" book with examples.

3409. DUBEY, Vinod. "The Marketed Agricultural Surplus and Economic Growth in Underdeveloped Countries," The Economic Journal, 73 (292):689, December, 1963.

3410. KRISHNA, Raj. "Farm Supply Response in India-Pakistan: A Case of the Punjah Region," The Economic Journal, 73(291):477, September, 1963.

3411. MATHUR, P.N., and EZEKIEL, H. "Marketable Surplus of Food and Price Fluctuations in a Developing Economy," Kyklos, (3):396, 1961.

3412. *SORENSON, Vernon L, (ed.). Agricultural Market Analysis. East Lansing: Michigan State University Press, 1964. 344 pp. Bibliographical footnotes.

3413. STERN, Robert M. "The Price Responsiveness of Primary Producers," Review of Economics and Statistics, 64(2):202, May, 1962.
Stern's conclusion is that the price system seems to work even in developing countries where peasant producers rely on rather primitive methods of production. Farmers do respond to changes in the price of the commodities they produce.

Other items that deal with Food and Agriculture are:

3001, 3103, 3110, 3130, 3139, 3123, 3135, 3144, 3207, 3214, 3216, 3218, 3224, 4001, 4002, 4004, 4103, 5004, 5527, 5551, 5553, 5561, 6001, 6602, 6615

Most all series 4100 and 4200 items apply to this section also.

3900. Bibliographies

3901. ABBOTT, John C. "Information Sources on Foreign Marketing," Journal of Marketing, 25(3):42, January, 1961.
A review of the main international reference sources of marketing.

3902. LINDFORS, Grace V. (ed.). Bibliography;Cases and other Materials For the Teaching of Multinational Business. Cambridge, Mass: Harvard University, 1964. 283 pp.
The major focus of the items chosen for this publication was multinational business. Annotations are given for most all items.

3903. MULVIHILL, Donald F. (ed.). Bibliography on Domestic Marketing Systems Abroad.(Bureau of Economic and Business Research, Printed Series No. 2.) Kent, Ohio: Kent State University, 1962. 68 pp.
The author asked for assistance from other countries. As he admits, the coverage is spotty,particularly so regarding Colombia and some other Latin countries. However, every entry is annotated and as such is of use to the international marketer.

3904. *STEWART, Charles F., and SIMMONS, George B. A Bibliography of International Business. New York: Columbia University Press, 1964. 603 pp.
A very comprehensive bibliography which includes over 5,000 items.

Other items that deal with Bibliographies are:

2108, 2114, 2117, 3156, 3224, 4008, 4103, 4116, 4204, 5551, 6003, 6021

In addition see other bibliographical sections.

CHAPTER 4 AGRICULTURE

4000 SERIES

4000. Miscellaneous

4001. BROWN, Lester R. Man, Land, and Food Looking Ahead at World Food Needs. (Foreign Agricultural Economics Report No. 11.) Washington, D.C.: USDA, Economic Research Service, Regional Analysis Division, November, 1963. 153 pp. Bibliography.

4002. CHAVES, Fernando. "The Agricultural Cooperative Movement in Latin America." Washington, D.C.: Pan American Union, October 17, 1962. (Mimeographed.)

__________. "Cooperative Education in Latin America." Washington, D.C.: Pan American Union, October 10, 1962. (Mimeographed.)

__________. "El Movemento Cooperativista En Americalatina." Washington, D.C.: Pan American Union, April 16, 1964. (Mimeographed.)

The author believes in cooperatives. Copies of the papers are available from him.

4003. CONKLIN, Harold C. "The Study of Shifting Cultivation," Current Anthropology, 2(1): 27, February, 1961.

4004. Cooperative Thrift, Credit and Marketing in Economically Undeveloped Countries. (FAO Development Paper, No. 34.) Roma, Italy, 1959. (First printed in July, 1953.) 63 pp.

Another "how to" paper for leaders in the agricultural sector.

4005. Food Aid and Other Forms of Utilization of Agricultural Surpluses, A Review of Programs, Principles and Consultations. Rome: Food and Agriculture Organization, 1964.

This paper deals with the subject of raising food consumption and levels of agricultural development by the use of surpluses in the less developed areas of the world.

4006. *Freedom From Hunger Campaign, Basic Studies. Rome: Food and Agriculture Organization

Basic Study #	Date	Title
2	1961	"Development through Food" (A Strategy for Surplus Utilization)
3	1962	"National Development Efforts"
5	1962	"Nutrition and Working Efficiency"
7	1962	"Population & Food Supply"
8	1962	"Aspects of Economic Development" (The Background to Freedom from Hunger)
10	1963	"Possibilities of Increasing World Food Production"

These six monographs provide excellent background information.

4007. GORST, Sheila. Cooperative Organization in Tropical Countries. Oxford, England: Basil Blackwell, 1959. 343 pp. Bibliography

A descriptive study of co-ops in British colonies.

4008. HARDIN, Charles M. (ed.). "Agricultural Policy, Politics, and the Public Interest," The Annals of the American Academy, 331, September, 1960.

4009. JOSEPHSON, Edward S. _Food Research and Development Freedom From Want_. (Industrial College of the Armed Forces Thesis, No. 76.) Washington D.C., March 30, 1962. 95 pp. Bibliography.

A description of technologically feasible ideas to increase the supply of food.

4010. MEHREN, G.L. "The Contribution of Industrial Development to Agricultural Development: Emphasis on Product Markets." A paper presented at a Social Science Research Conference. Stanford, California, November, 1960.

"The basic objective of this paper is to relate changes in growth, composition, and distribution of income to changes in organization and operation of markets for farm products . . . . This paper is pitched at a case-studies level reflecting limited field experience and the absence of testable theory and of data."

4011. _Report of the World Food Congress_. Washington D.C., June 4-8, 1963. Rome: Food and Agriculture Organization, 1963.

One of the facts mentioned is that during the last decade income in the less developed countries grew at the rate of about 3 percent a year. But the increase per caput was only U.S. $1, as against U.S. $20 in the advanced countries. There are many interesting reports in the resume.

4012. THOMPSON, John. "The Fisheries Industry of El Salvador," _Journal of Inter-American Studies_, 8(3):437, July, 1961.

Dr. Thompson suggests that the fisheries industry serves primarily upper income consumers. He believes that the industry has significant possibilities for development.

4013. ________. "La Industria Lechera de Chile Central," _Informaciones Geograficas_, (Santiago, Chile), Numero Unica, 8-23, 1957.

4014. ________. "Production, Marketing, and Consumption of Cattle in El Salvador," The Professional Geographer, 8(5):1, September, 1961.
The article consists of a descriptive report of the cattle industry in 1959 followed by conclusions of the likelihood of change.

Other items that deal with Miscellaneous are:

1710, 3002, 3012, 3401, 3405, 3406, 3408, 3409, 3410, 3412, 5508, 5554, 5558, 5706, 5805, 5901

4100. Area Studies

4101. ALEXANDER, Robert J. "Nature and Progress of Agrarian Reform in Latin America," Journal of Economic History, 23(4):559, December, 1963.

4102. ANDERSON, A.W., and BEJARANO, J. La Industria de Carne en Colombia. Bogota: Ferrocarriles Nacionales de Colombia, 1961. 53 pp.

4103. *Inter American Committee for Agricultural Development (CIDA). Inventory of Information Basic to the Planning of Agricultural Development in Latin America, Regional Report. Washington D.C.: Pan American Union, October, 1963. 202 pp. Bibliographical footnotes.

This study is, as the title states, an inventory. The conclusion of the chapter on marketing is indicative of the needs. In that chapter, the author has done a country-by-country analysis ; one of the conclusions is: "Although there is considerable talk about inefficient and expensive marketing, marketing is, in fact, a neglected field in Latin America. Objective analyses are needed of the processes employed and the expenses incurred in providing each country with food and other products of agricultural origin. Very few studies of this type have been encountered except for reports by FAO marketing specialists working in northeastern Brazil and in Chile."

The principal subjects studied were:

a. Quantitative and qualitative information regarding agriculture development.
b. Levels of consumption and demand.
c. Natural resources.
d. Uses of land and agricultural production.
e. Land tenure.
f. Human resources.
g. Agricultural institutions
h. Agricultural income; the micro-economy.

i. Agricultural capital and credit.
j. Price studies.
k. Marketing.
l. Taxes.
m. Functions of the State in agricultural development.

The book gives an idea of both answers and lack of answers that are available in each area. See next item 4104 for an example of the country studies that are available for each of the Latin American Republics.

4104. *Inter-American Committee for Agricultural Development. Inventory of Information Basic to the Planning of Agricultural Development in Latin America. Brazil. Washington, D.C.: Pan American Union, December, 1964. 156 pp. Bibliographical footnotes.

This is one of a series of books about the available information on various aspects of agriculture in each country of Latin America. These handbooks should be on the reference shelf of any researcher concerned with agricultural aspects of economic development. All the country studies were published in 1963 and 1964.

4105. LASTRA, C.J. The Development of Puerto Rico as Related to the Development of Latin America. Puerto Rico: Department of Commerce, April, 1962.

4106. ________. Importancia del Mercado Local para la Industriá Puertoriquena. Puerto Rico: Department of Commerce, January, 1963.

4107. PARKS, R.W. "The Role of Agriculture in Mexican Economic Development," Inter-American Economic Affairs, 18(1):3, Summer, 1964.

Major features of Mexican agricultural development from 1925 to 1960 are stressed. The author concludes that agriculture has contributed. Bibliography stresses methodology.

4108. *POSADA, Antonio J. "Economics of Colombian Agriculture." Unpublished Ph.D. dissertation, University of Wisconsin, 1952.

The author, a native of Colombia, writes mainly from his own experience. This excellent study is now somewhat dated, but could be quite useful as a benchmark.

"In conclusion it may be said that: (1) Except for certain staple commodities which are largely exported, there is a lack of organization of the marketing structure . . . (2) Farmers have few, often no, alternative outlets for their products. (3) Transportation facilities are inadequate, costly, and give poor service. (4) Storage, especially refrigerated storage, is totally inadequate. (5) Pricing is done on the most antiquated basis. (6) Marketing margins are wide."

4109. RILEY, Harold M. "Beef Production in Colombia." Palmira, Colombia, 1962. (Mimeographed.) 125 pp. Bibliography.

This report is a part of a major research undertaking. It will likely be published in book form under the title of _Long Term Projections of Supply and Demand for Selected Agricultural Products in Colombia_.

4110. ________. "Facilities for the Processing of Agricultural Products in Colombia." A section from an unpublished report on marketing of agricultural products in Colombia. (Mimeographed.) 1961.

4111. STEWART, Sir H., _et al._ _The Agricultural Development of Colombia_. Report of a Mission organized by the International Bank for Reconstruction and Development. 1956. See pp. 124-138; 315-330.

4112. THOMPSON, John. "Studies in the Food Supply of El Salvador." Report of Field Work carried out under office of Naval

Research Contract 222 (11) NR 388 067. Berkeley: Department of Geography, University of California, 1961. (Mimeographed.) 64 pp.

The report is separated on the basis of commodities. Dr. Thompson discusses production and distribution of cereals and beans, fruits and vegetables, beef and dairy, and swine.

4113. USDA. <u>The 1964 Western Hemisphere Agricultural Situation</u>. ERS-Foreign, No. 71 (February, 1964).

4114. USDA. <u>The World Food Budget, 1962 and 1966</u>. (Foreign Agricultural Economic Report, No. 4. October, 1961. 78 pp.

4115. WARD, Barbara E. "Cash or Credit Crops? An Examination of Some Implications of Peasant Commercial Production with Special Reference to the Multiplicity of Traders and Middlemen," <u>Economic Development and Cultural Change</u>, 8(2):148, January, 1960.

The article argues that the plethora of middlemen in underdeveloped countries serves the function of supplying much-needed credit for daily subsistence and for big purchases by the peasants. The multiplicity of middlemen stems from the fact that all credit relationships are intensely personal. There appears to be a hierarchy of credit relationships, with small middlemen getting credit from larger middlemen. With regard to productivity, a side effect of the credit structure is that being constantly in debt motivates peasants to produce for cash when they might otherwise produce only for subsistence.

4116. WHARTON, Clifton R., Jr. "Recent Trends of Output and Efficiency in the Agricultural Production of Brazil, Minas Gerais, and Sao Paulo," <u>Inter-American Economic Affairs</u>, 13(2):60, Autumn, 1959.

Other items that deal with Area Studies are:

1105, 1156, 1703, 2011, 2015, 2101, 2108, 2110, 2116, 2117, 2602, 3002, 3207, 3210, 3214, 3216, 3218, 3224, 3402, 3401, 3405, 5009, 5528, 5710, 5712, 5722, 5728, 6013

In addition, many of the series 3100 and 4200 items apply to this section.

4200. Economic Development

4201. "Agriculture in Economic Development," Monthly Bulletin of Agricultural Economics and Statistics, 13(2):1, February, 1964.

The article notes five main aspects of agriculture's contribution to economic progress. It concludes with a review of interrelations between agricultural and industrial development and a discussion of the role of planning in accelerating economic development.

4202. BARLOWE, R. "Land Reform and Economic Development," Journal of Farm Economics, 35(2):173, May, 1953.

"In conclusion, emphasis might well be placed on the point that land reform by itself provides no guarantee of economic development . . . even under ideal circumstances it must be recognized that land reform cannot do the job alone. Other programs must be used in conjunction with land reform."

Another overview of land reform.

4203. *EICHER, Carl K., and WITT, Lawrence W. (eds.). Agriculture in Economic Development. New York: McGraw Hill, 1964. 415 p. Bibliography.

This is an extensive book of readings on the relationship between agriculture and economic development. It should be a part of one's library.

4204. *"Factors Associated with Differences and Changes in Agricultural Production in Underdeveloped Countries." Development and Trade Analysis Division, United States Department of Agriculture. January, 1965. (Mimeographed.) 21 pp.

This paper is the third semi-annual research report to the Agency for International Development. If additional information is needed, the team director,

Mr. Wade Gregory, can be contacted. The first published report on this work is expected to be available from the Department of Agriculture in mid-1965.

4205. FAO-INA. Estudios presentados en las Jornadas Latinoamericanas de Comercializacion de Productos Agricolas, Bogota, Abril-Junio de 1961. Bogota, Colombia: Institute Nacional de Abastecimientos (INA), 1962.
It includes twenty papers on various aspects of agricultural development.

4206. HAROLDSEN, E.O. (ed.). Food, One Tool in International Economic Development. Ames, Iowa: Iowa State University Press, 1962.
A compilation of twenty papers presented at a seminar in February, 1962. Near the end of the book quotes from each article appear in a twelve-page overview.

4207. HAVENS, A. Eugene. "El Combia en la Technologia Agricola de Subachoque," in Factors Sociales que Inciden en el Desarrollo Economico de la Hoya del Rio Subachoque. Bogota, Colombia: Facultad de Sociologia, Universidad Nacional de Colombia, 1963.

4208. HOLMBERG, Allan R. "Land Tenure and Planned Social Change: A Case Study from Vicos, Peru," Human Organization, 18(1):7, Spring, 1959.
An article on the Vicos project.
See other Henry Dobyns or Allan Holmberg articles.

4209. JACOBY, Erich H. Inter-relationship Between Agrarian Reform and Agricultural Development. (FAO Studies No. 26.) Rome: Food and Agriculture Organization. Sept., 1953. 64 pp.
An overview of what land reform is and what it does. Marketing plays a part in making a more efficient system.

4210. JOHNSON, Sherman E. "Potential Contributions of Agriculture to Economic Growth in Less Developed Countries," The Annals of the American Academy, 331:52, September, 1960.

4211. JOHNSTON, Bruce F., and MELLOR, J.W. "The Role of Agriculture in Economic Development," American Economic Review, 51(4): 565, September, 1961.

4212. *SCHULTZ, Theodore W. Transforming Traditional Agriculture. New Haven: Yale University Press, 1964. 212 pp. Bibliographical footnotes.

Is it true that the economics which has grown up in the U.S. and Western Europe is of no use in analyzing problems in the new countries? Are traditional farmers stupid? Dr. Schultz says no in both cases and gives interesting reasons for so doing.

4213. *STEVENS, Robert D. Elasticity of Food Consumption Associated with Changes in Income in Developing Countries. (Foreign Agricultural Economic Report No. 23.) Washington, D.C.: U.S. Department of Agriculture, March, 1965. 85 pp. Tables, Charts, Bibliography.

This pioneering economic study was undertaken to provide some better understanding of food consumption in the developing nations. Dr. Stevens felt that this study could provide more precise information on the relation of income changes and food consumption changes. This knowledge could then be used to provide better understanding of future food needs.

In the "highlights" of the study, Dr. Stevens notes that "an Engel Curve for food was derived from consumption data for many countries. The results of this analysis provide evidence that the income elasticity of total food consumption per capita must range between .9 and .4 . . . (but) the usual range for this elasticity appears to be between .6 and .8." He also suggests that during the early phases of development process, nations are likely to experience a 5% per annum rate of growth in food requirements.

This study provides one of the few guidelines for how rapidly demand for food will increase. The author discusses such topics as: "Measures of food," "Importance of food at retail as income rises," and "Examples of rates of increase in food requirements during development." He has also four appendices which provide detailed information on both his methodology and the subject area. Dr. Stevens'study could well become a landmark in its area.

4214. Technology and Economic Development," _Scientific American_, 209(3):entire issue, September, 1963.

Brief essays by specialists on the developing nations. Many charts and diagrams included. Specific case studies are also highlighted. Some of the articles are: "Technology and Economic Development," "Population," "Food," "Water," "Energy," "Minerals," "Education for Development," "The Structure of Development," "The Development of Brazil," and "The Planning of Development."

4215. U.S. Department of Agriculture, ERS. _Agriculture and Economic Growth_, (Agricultural Economic Report, No. 28.) 1963.

4216. WHARTON, Clifton R., Jr. "The Economic Meaning of 'Subsistence,'" _Maylayan Economic Review_, 8(2):46, October, 1963.

An excellent article which gives a more precise meaning to the term "subsistence". Reprints of this article can be obtained from Publications Secy., Agricultural Development Council, Inc., 630 Fifth Ave., New York 20, New York.

Other items that deal with Economic Development are:

2015, 2101, 2104, 2108, 2110, 2116, 2117, 2602, 2808, 2901, 3401, 3405, 3406, 4101, 4103, 4105, 4107, 4112, 4901, 5554, 5556, 5712, 5715, 5801, 5805, 6013, 6014, 6605, 6614

See Series 3100, 3200 and 4000 also.

4900. Bibliographies

4901. *"Bibliography; Agrarian Reform and Tenure." Land Tenure Center Library, University of Wisconsin, August, 1964. (Mimeographed.) 78 pp.

The preface states that the bibliography "is a moderately selective collection of what is most recent and found to be most valuable . . . . Its focus is agrarian reform and tenure, rather than the broader subject of economic development."

4902. *"Bibliography of the Cornell Peru Project, 1951-1962." Department of Anthropology, Cornell University, December, 1962. 15 pp.

Another name for this ongoing effort is "Vicos Project." It is a joint effort between Cornell and the National Indian Institute of Peru in applied anthropology. The studies have ranged over a wide variety of areas. See other items concerning this project written by Henry F. Dobyns and/or Allan Holmberg.

4903. *FAO Bibliography of Food and Agricultural Marketing. Rome: Food and Agriculture Organization, United Nations. (Mimeographed.)

Begun in 1950, this is probably the most comprehensive bibliography in agricultural marketing. It is kept up-to-date by annual supplements.

4904. A Selected Bibliography on Agricultural Productivity in Underdeveloped Countries. Cambridge, Mass.: Center for International Studies, M.I.T., 1964. (Lithographed.)

An annotated bibliography of interest that was compiled for the summer study on increasing agricultural productivity in underdeveloped countries. It has only five items on marketing.

4905. The State of Food and Agriculture, 1964. Rome: Food and Agriculture Organization of the United Nations, 1964.

This is an annual publication loaded with statistics.

"FAO's latest indices of agricultural production confirm that, in contrast to earlier increases in per capita production, for five years now world agricultural production has done no more than keep up with the annual population growth of about 2%."

Other items that deal with Bibliographies are:

2101, 2114, 3210, 3214, 3216, 3218, 3224, 3401, 3403, 3405, 3407, 3411, 4101, 4103, 5508, 5511, 5805, 6603

See also the other bibliographical sections.

CHAPTER 5 COMMUNICATIONS

5000 SERIES

5000. Miscellaneous

5001. BARNETT, Homer G. "Anthropology as an Applied Science," Human Organization, 17(1):9, Spring, 1958.

5002. BENNETT, J.W. "Cross-Cultural Research & The Study of National Acculturation," a chapter from Some Uses of Anthropology. The Anthropological Society, Joseph B. Casogrande and Thomas Gladwin (eds.). Washington, D.C.: The Anthropological Society, 1956. 120 pp. Bibliography.

5003. COUCH, Carl J. "Communication and Change." Preliminary draft, publication No. 9. Institute for Extension Personnel Development, Michigan State University, April, 1964.

5004. DAMLE, Y.B. "Communication of Modern Ideas and Knowledge in Indian Villages." Cambridge, Massachusetts: MIT Center for International Studies, 1955.

The author studied seven Indian villages with various degrees of isolation from Poona City. The seven villages were chosen so as to form a scale along the continuum of communication distance from an urban center. Villages ranged from one to eighty miles from Poona. He interviewed only a few non-randomly chosen respondents in each village.

5005. DEUTSCHMANN, Paul J. "The Efficiency of Different Modes of Communication," Audio-Visual Communication Review, 10(3):176, May-June, 1962.

5006. ________. "A Machine Simulation of Attitude Change in a Polarized Community." Programa, Interamericano De Informacion Popular, San Jose, Costa Rica, September 21, 1962. (Mimeographed.)

5007. ________. "The Mass Media in an Underdeveloped Village," Journalism Quarterly, 40 (1):27, Winter, 1963.

"Even at the low level of a small Andean village there are persons receiving messages from the modern mass media. The study suggests the process of media audience building may be fundamentally the same in this quite different culture (Saucio, Colombia) as in the U.S."

5008. ________, MCNELLY, John T., and ELLINGSWORTH, Huber. "Mass Media Use by Sub-Elites in Eleven Latin American Countries," Journalism Quarterly, 38(4):460, Autumn, 1961.

Daily use of mass media by Latin American professional and technical people was found to be roughly on a par with that of comparable North Americans.

5009. DIAZ-B.,Juan. Sociological and Psychological Factors Related to the Search for Instrumental Information Among Farmers of the Brazilian Northeast. First Interamerican Research Symposium on the Role of Communications in Agricultural Development. Mexico City, Mexico, October 5-13, 1964.

5010. *GEIGER, Theodore and SOLOMON, Leo. Motivations and Methods in Development and

Foreign Aid. Proceedings of the Sixth World Conference of the Society for International Development. Washington, D.C., March 16-18, 1964. 152 pp.

The conference proceedings of this recently formed professional group should be of interest to development experts. The Society for International Development is interdisciplinary and one of its purposes is to enable persons interested in development to have a forum for exchange of ideas.

5011. HAVENS, A. Eugene. "Some Theoretical and Methodological Considerations for Research on Diffusion in Latin America," Paper presented at the Society for Applied Anthropology. San Juan, Puerto Rico, 1964.

5012. MCNELLY, John T., and DEUTSCHMANN, Paul J. "Media Use and Socio-economic Status in a Latin American Capital," Gazette, 9(1):1, 1963. Bibliography.

There was found to be a "strong relationship between mass media consumption and the socio-economic status of individuals. But really socio-economic level and media use are intertwined as causal factors in the diffusion of information."

5013. *PYE, Lucian W. (ed.). Communications and Political Development. Princeton, N.J.: Princeton University Press, 1963. 381 pp. Bibliography.

A collection of revisions of papers originally prepared for the Conference on Communication and Political Development held in 1961.

The editor has written an introduction to each paper and thereby strengthened the continuity.

5014. WHITEFORD, Andrew H. Two Cities of Latin America: A Comparative Description of Social Classes. Garden City, New York: Doubleday Anchor Book, 1964 edition.

266 pp. Bibliography.

This comparative description of social class in Popayan, Colombia, and Queretaro, Mexico, was undertaken during the early fifties. The book was first published by Beloit College in 1960. It details the criteria for membership in all parts of the social structure. Even in a very traditional society like the one that exists in Popayan, Whiteford finds a middle class.

Other items that deal with Communications are:

1105, 2008, 2014, 2601, 2602, 2603, 2902, 2905, 3004, 3013, 3133, 4008, 4205, 4207, 4208, 4903, 6001, 6005, 6006, 6007, 6010, 6024, 6601, 6603, 6617, 6832, 6833, 6905

5500. Invention, Innovation and Entrepreneurship

5501. *BARNETT, Homer G. Innovation: The Basis of Cultural Change. New York: McGraw-Hill, 1953. 462 pp.

One of the few theoretical discussions of innovation and social change is presented in this well-written book.

5502. BOULDING, Kenneth. "Religious Foundations of Economic Progress," Harvard Business Review, 30(3):33, May-June, 1952.

Dr. Boulding reviews the essential factors for economic development. (1) Innovation must occur. (2) Imitation must take place. (3) Displacement results. (4) Capital must be accumulated. (5) Population must be limited.

5503. COCHRAN, Thomas C. "Cultural Factors in Economic Growth," Journal of Economic History, 20(4): 515, December, 1960.

An analysis of the character of Latin individuals and Latin American culture. The author attempts to relate this character to the rate and direction of economic progress in the area.

5504. COLE, Arthur H. Business Enterprise in its Social Setting. Cambridge, Massachusetts: Harvard University Press, 1959. 286 pp. Bibliography.

This is a classic on the role of the entrepreneur. Cole synthesizes in the second part of his book the research at Harvard.

5505. COLLINS, Orvis F., et al. The Enterprising Man. East Lansing, Michigan: Michigan State University Press, 1964. 254 pp.

A study of about 100 entrepreneurs in Michigan. Collins, a disciple of Lloyd Warner, uses typical Warner techniques. In addition, he compares his findings with those of earlier Warnerian studies of big business leaders. He found many differences between big business leaders and entrepreneurs.

5506. CORSON, John J. "Innovation Challenges Conformity," <u>Harvard Business Review</u>, 40(3):67, May/June, 1962.

5507. *DIAMOND, H.S. "Studies in Innovation Theory." Unpublished Ph.D. dissertation, Columbia University, 1951. (University Microfilms No. 2807.)

The author's purpose is "the examination of the process of innovation together with some of its economic and social attributes." He suggests, though, that it is difficult to categorize causes of innovation but one can talk of innovations' consequences.

Diamond considers invention and innovation part of the same process. He believes some inventions will succeed more rapidly than others because they do not compete with established ways of doing things.

There are, in this thesis, many seminal ideas.

5508. DOBYNS, Henry F., MONGE, M. Carlos, and VAZQUEZ, Mario V. "Summary of Technical-Organizational Progress and Reactions to It," <u>Human Organization</u>, 21(2):109, Summer, 1962.

A summary of the results of ten years' work on that interesting and effective innovation in social change in Peru, the Vicos project. See other citations from Dobyns and from Holmberg.

5509. HAGEN, Everett E. "The Entrepreneur as Rebel against Traditional Society," <u>Human Organization</u>, 19(4):185, Winter, 1960-61.

Industrialization depends in part upon entrepreneurs. The values of a given society may hinder or promote such development. This article presents some observations on Colombian entrepreneurs.

Hagen points out that the attitude of the traditionalist in Latin America toward business is somewhat like that in the mid-western small town where he grew up. "The saloon keeper in my midwestern town made more money than any businessman with his capacity in that town. But a decent person did not go into this business and did not want that money."

Hagen then presents an effective argument for the concept of the businessman as rebel. (He develops it more thoroughly in his 1962 book.)

5510. HIRSCHMEIER, Johannes, S.V.D. The Origins of Entrepreneurship in Meizi Japan. Cambridge: Harvard University Press, 1964. 354 pp. Bibliography.

This is an attempt to integrate the writing of a general history of Meizi industrial development and present studies of the entrepreneurs who themselves were major actors in that period.

In the conclusion Hirschmeier says: "The most important resource for development is the will to succeed," and "A man cannot be compartmentalized--he cannot easily be a changed man economically and remain socially and otherwise tradition-bound."

5511. HOLMBERG, Allan R. "Changing Community Attitudes and Values in Peru, A Case Study in Guided Change," Social Change in Latin America Today. New York: Council on Foreign Relations, 1960.

The Vicos project. See other citations by Holmberg.

5512. *KRIESBERG, L. "Entrepreneurs in Latin America and the Role of Cultural and Situational Processes," International Social Science Journal, 15(4):581, 1963.

Late in the article he notes a number of hypotheses. Among them are the following:

H_1 Behavior begun early in life cycle is particularly dependent upon parental influence. Such things as Diet and Basic Educ. skills

H_2 Behavior which is not independent of previous behavior is more likely to be determined by cultural processes than behavior which is serially independent.

H_3 Behavior differs in the degree to which its results are subject to testing. If behavior is not unique, a person has a greater chance to experiment and learn from his own experience.

5513. LARSEN, Otto N. "Innovators and Early Adopters of Televisions," Sociological Inquiry, 32(1):16, Winter, 1962.

5514. MANSFIELD, Edwin. "Intrafirm Rates of Diffusion of an Innovation," Review of Economics and Statistics, 45(4):348, November, 1963.

5515. ________. "Size of Firm, Market Structure and Innovation," Journal of Political Economy, 71(6):556, December, 1963.

5516. MASON, Robert. "The Use of Information Sources by Influentials In the Adoption Process," Public Opinion Quarterly, 27:455, Fall, 1963.

5517. MASSELL, Benton F. "Capital Formation and Technological Change in United States Manufacturing," Review of Economics and Statistics, 62(2):182, May, 1960.

He attempts to apportion increases in output per man-hour between increases in capital employed per man-hour and that nebulous constellation of forces called technological change. Thus one can then suggest "what proportion of our investment resources should be devoted to improving the technology, rather than to expanding existing types of capital equipment and structures."

5518. ________. "Investment, Innovation and Growth," Econometrica, 30(2):239, April, 1962.

This paper builds upon his earlier one in RESTAT. It "considers this technological relationship between investment and technical progress, in the context of a highly simplified model."

In the future, investment might become the more important of the two; but the historical evidence shows that although investment and innovation are interrelated, innovation is much more important.

5519. *MAYNARD, Geoffrey. Economic Development and the Price Level. London: MacMillan, 1962. 295 pp. Bibliography.

An interesting book for students of development.

"Savers in under-developed countries seem to be reluctant to lose direct control over their wealth, and prefer to invest it in a manner which leaves it in their possession . . . the basic cause of unproductive investment may well be the absence of an entrepreneurial or capitalist class which thinks in terms of re-investing its income productivity for future income rather than capital gain."

5520. MENZEL, Herbert, KATZ, Elihu, and COLEMAN, James. "The Diffusion of an Innovation Among Physicians," Sociometry, 20(4): 253, December, 1957.

5521. MERRILL, R.S. "Routine Innovation." Unpublished Ph.D. dissertation, University of Chicago, December, 1959. (University of Chicago Microfilm No. 4877.)

Routine innovation equals learning, by Merrill's definition. Routine innovations are thus defined as innovations which are produced by the use of culturally learned skills. There are acts of skills and acts of insight.

5522. *MEYER, H.H., WALKER, Wm. B., and LETWIN, G.H. "Motive Patterns and Risk Preferences Associated with Entrepreneurship," Journal of Abnormal Psychology, 63(3):570-574, September, 1961. Bibliography.

Excellent article reviewing Need-Achievement work and studies.

Study of entrepreneurs and specialists at G.E. only partially validated McClelland and Atkinson's work on the achievement motive.

5523. *National Bureau of Economic Research. The Rate and Direction of Inventive Activity: Economic and Social Factors. Princeton: Princeton University Press, 1962.

A Conference of the Universities--National Bureau Committee for Economic Research and the Committee on Economic Growth of the Social Science Research Council held in 1960. This conference focused on invention.

5524. PAULSEN, Andreas. "Entrepreneurs and Entrepreneurial Activities in Developing Countries," Jabrbucher fur Nationalokonome, und Statistik, 175(5):385, December, 1963.

The study examines whether the entrepreneurial activity according to Schumpeter is of theoretical and practical importance for developing countries.

5525. SCHON, Donald A. "Champions For Radical New Inventions," Harvard Business Review, 41 (2):77, March, 1963.

5526. ________. "How Companies Strangle Innovation," Management Review, 52:44, September, 1963.

5527. SHETTY, M.C. "Entrepreneurship in Small Industry," International Development Review, 6(2), June, 1964.

This paper was one of several presented at the first SID Regional Conference in Calcutta, India, February 15-16, 1964.

Here in this article are only some highlights. For instance: "This paper seeks to emphasize the role of "imitative" as opposed to "innovative" entrepreneur-managers in the newly industrialized countries." Shetty argues that the Schumpeterian entrepreneur has been "almost rendered superfluous" because of planned development.

5528. "Social Research in Latin America," The American Behavioral Scientist, 8 (1), September, 1964 (Special Issue).
Frank Joy Moreno and Rodman C. Rockefeller are the editors of this special issue. The issue can be purchased from American Behavioral Scientist, 80 E. 11th Street, New York.

5529. SOLOW, Robert M. "Technical Change and the Aggregate Production Function," Review of Economics and Statistics, 39(3):312, August, 1957.

5530. *STRASSMAN, W. Paul. Risk and Technological Innovation. Ithaca, New York: Cornell University, 1959. 249 pp. Bibliography.
Strassman argues that innovation was rampant in the late nineteenth century because of lack of worker and government opposition.

Other items that deal with Invention, Innovation and Entrepreneurship are:

1701, 1709, 2116, 3004, 3013, 3110, 3133, 3146, 3156, 3213, 4103, 4902, 5006, 5008, 5012, 5703, 5705, 5708, 5711, 5713, 5716, 5902, 5905, 6603, 6608, 6614, 6615, 6618, 6817

Note that the items of series 5550 and 5800 have considerable overlap with this area.

5550. Diffusion of Innovations

5551. BYLUND, H. Bruce. Social and Psychological Factors Associated with Acceptance of New Food Products. (Pennsylvania State University Agricultural Experiment Station Bulletin, No. 708.) University Park, Pennsylvania: December, 1963. 30 pp.

5552. *DAHLING, Randall L. "Shannon's Information Theory, The Spread of an Idea," in Studies of Innovation and of Communication to the Public. Elihu Katz, et. al. (See #5558.)

Dahling, in this most interesting article, traces the diffusion of Shannon's theory into various academic fields. As a result of his study, Dahling concludes that perceived need is correlated with the rapidity of the adoption of an innovation.

5553. DEUTSCHMANN, Paul J., and MENDEZ, A.D. "Adoption of New Foods and Drugs in Cholina: A Preliminary Report." San Jose, Costa Rica: PIIP & INCAP, November, 1962. (Mimeographed.)

5554. GRILICHES, Zvi. "Hybrid Corn: An Exploration in the Economics of Technological Change," Econometrica, 25(4):501, October, 1957.

This is an economist's attempt to explain diffusion. E.M. Rogers and Griliches have had a running battle on this issue. (See Rural Sociology, 25: 354; and 27:325 for elaboration.)

5555. HAVENS, A. Eugene. "La Adopcion de Innovaciones Una Comparacion entre Colombia y Estados Unidos," Memoria del Primer Congreso Nacional de Sociologia. Bogota: Asociacion Colombiana de Sociologia, 1963.

5556. HOCHSTRASSER, Donald L. "Possum Ridge Farmers: A Study in Cultural Change." Unpublished Ph.D.

dissertation, University of Oregon, 1963. (University Microfilms No. 63-4255.)

Hochstrasser makes distinctions between "thinking and feeling" and "doing and acting." This study attempted to determine why certain persons tended to be non-adopters and determined that the main reason was that it was economically not feasible.

Most agriculture innovations were not new or novel to the respondents. "The conception of farm adoption as a series of events from "becoming aware of," to "trial of," so-called innovations or new and improved methods is an unrealistic one. It fails to recognize the existence on the farmer's part of knowledge and ideas about different and competitive means of farming. The author argues that diffusion must be treated both as a process and a result.

5557. KATZ, Elihu, HAMILTON, Herbert, and LEVIN, Martin L. "Traditions of Research on the Diffusion of Innovation," American Sociological Review, 28(1):237, April, 1963.

5558. *KATZ, Elihu, et al. Studies of Innovation and of Communication to the Public. (Studies in the Utilization of Behavioral Science, Vol. II.) Stanford, California: Institute for Communication Research, Stanford University, 1962: 286 pp.

Included within the covers of this book are several interesting studies. The first paper by Katz compares and contrasts the adoption of hybrid seed corn with a new drug. Katz defines a diffusion study as one tracing the movement of a given new practice; that is, over time through specific channels of communication and within a social structure.

Some of the other studies are E. A. Wilkening's "The Communication of Ideas on Innovation in Agriculture"; E. M. Rogers on characteristics of types of farmers; and Robert Mason who suggests that there are only two necessary and sufficient conditions for adoption, "awareness" and "adoption."

5559. KLONGLAN, Gerald. "Role of a Free-Sample Offer in the Adoption of a Technological Innovation." Unpublished Ph.D. dissertation, Iowa State University, 1963.

5560. KOLARS, John F. _Tradition Season, and Change in a Turkish Village_. (NAS-NRC Foreign Field Research Program Report No. 15.) Chicago: Department of Geography, Research Paper No. 83, University of Chicago, August, 1963.

A study of change in different Turkish communities. Three villages are studied intensively. The communities studied range from "backward" to "progressive." Yet about "fifty years ago each type of village closely resembled the other, but since that time change and development have given distinct characteristics. Some villages have altered very little and remain much as they were; other settlements have become more deeply involved in the market economy of the nation." The author attempts to isolate those variables which have contributed to this change.

In conclusion, he says, "It is impossible to trace such development back to a single cause . . . But, no commercial agriculture could have occurred without parallel or preceding growth of adequate systems of transportation and marketing."

5561. MASON, Robert G. "The Use of Information Sources in the Process of Adoption," _Rural Sociology_, 29(1):40, March, 1964.

5562. PARKER, William N., _et al_. _The Diffusion of Technical Knowledge as an Instrument of Economic Development_. (Symposia Series No. 13.) Washington, D.C.: The National Institute of Social and Behavioral Science, 1962.

This publication includes the presentations of the authors at a 1962 AAAS meeting. It is an excellent paper contributing toward a theory of diffusion.

5563. REHDER, Robert R. "The Role of the Detail Man in the Diffusion and Adoption of an

Ethical Pharmaceutical Innovation." Unpublished Ph.D. dissertation, Stanford University, 1961. (University Microfilms No. 61-1037.) 220 pp. Bibliography.

Rehder studies the business and professional aspects of the drug industry and the medical profession. He notes that "the interdependency of the ethical pharmaceutical industry and the medical profession appears to be increasing but that there are conflicting ethics which are becoming more apparent."

Rehder asks what actually is the influence of the detail man who has a new drug to promote. He follows four detail men through their introduction of the new drug, "Mensyn." He goes beyond the earlier work of Menzel and Katz and suggests that "there is some indication that he (the detail man) is able to by-pass opposing opinion leaders who might intefere with further transmission of mass media."

5564. *ROGERS, Everett M. The Diffusion of Innovations. New York: Free Press of Glencoe, 1962. 367 pp. Bibliography.

A review of hundreds of diffusion studies, concluding with some interesting suggestions for further research as well as statements on the state of the art of diffusion research. The book has an excellent bibliography.

5565. *TAX, Sol. Penny Capitalism: A Guatemalan Indian Economy. Chicago: University of Chicago Press, 1963. 230 pp. Bibliography.

This is the intensive report of one Indian community. There was in the economy an ethic which made business ventures socially acceptable. But, he asked if pure competition maximized welfare, and concluded it did not.

Here is a region closely approximating Adam Smith's description of pure competition which was terribly poor. Tax concluded it was because of inferior technology. He felt that individuals could not increase wealth of that society unless they have something with which to increase it. This is one of the classics of economic anthropology.

5566. "What Opinion do Opinion Leaders Lead?," Printers Ink, 286:11, January 10, 1964.

Other items that deal with Diffusion of Innovations are:

1704, 1714, 2014, 2601, 3133, 4208, 5005, 5006, 5007, 5012, 5705, 5715, 5716, 5717, 5726, 5905, 6009, 6018, 6022, 6023, 6024, 6606, 6609, 6013, 6618, 6832, 6833, 6904, 6905

Note that the items of 5500 and 5800 have considerable overlap with this area.

5700. Social Change

5701. AHUMADA, Jorge. "Hypothesis for the Diagnosis of a Situation of Social Change. The Case of Venezuela," International Social Science Journal, 16(2):192, 1964.

5702. ALERS-Montalvo, Manuel. "Cultural Change in a Costa Rican Village." Unpublished Ph.D. dissertation, Michigan State University, 1963. 185 pp.

5703. ARENSBERG, Conrad M., and NIEHOFF, Arthur H. Introducing Social Change, A Manual for Overseas Americans. Chicago: Aldine, 1964. 214 pp. Bibliography.

5704. BROWN, Murray, and DECANI, John S. "Technological Change and the Distribution of Income," International Economic Review, 4(3):289, September, 1963. Bibliographical footnotes.

5705. COHEN, E. "Stimulus Conditions as Factors in Social Change." Unpublished Ph.D. dissertation, University of Oklahoma, 1955. (University Microfilms No. 14,002.)

5706. DOBYNS, Henry F., and CARRASCO, Ella R. Un Analisis de la Situacion de las Comunidades Indigenas en el Ambiante Nacional. (Folletos del Proyecto Peru--Cornell No. 1.) Lima, Peru, 1962.
A description and analysis of the Vicos project.

5707. EISENSTADT, S.N. "Institutionalization and Change," American Sociological Review, 29 (2):235-247, April, 1964. Bibliographical footnotes.
"Just as the predilection for change is necessarily built into any institutional system, so the direction and scope of change are not random but depend . . . on

the nature of the system generating the change, on its values, norms and organizations, on the various internal forces operating within it and on the external forces to which it is especially sensitive because of its systematic properties . . . . A full explication of systematic sociological concepts can provide a fruitful initial step for the analysis of change."

An interesting article arguing for more social research into change.

5708. FOSTER, George M. Traditional Cultures, and the Impact of Technological Change. New York: Harper & Brothers, 1962. 292 pp. Bibliography.

Another of the excellent books by anthropologists on the culture and planned change. The second chapter, "How Cultures Change," and the last chapter, "The Ethics of Planned Change," are both especially good. Foster suggests at least some U.S. technical assistance has been,in essence, "if you people will learn to do more things the way we do them, you will be better off," and that such an attitude on the part of the U.S. is not very flattering.

5709. *GOODENOUGH, Ward H. Cooperation in Change. New York: Russell Sage Foundation, 1963. 543 pp. Bibliographical references.

Ostensibly Goodenough has written a book for change agents involved in community development. Actually the book should get a broader readership. It is an excellent source book for understanding change. Chapters twelve and thirteen are especially interesting to the marketing man.

5710. *HOLMBERG, Allan R. "The Changing Values and Institutions of Vicos in the Context of National Development," The American Behavioral Scientist, 8(7):3, March, 1965.

Another of the articles on the interesting case of applied social science. See

Index--Cornell-Peru Project. This entire issue of the ABS was devoted to the Vicos Case.

5711. ________, and DOBYNS, Henry F. "The Process of Accelerating Community Change," Human Organization, 21 (2):107, Summer, 1962.

"Early observation of the Vicos community . . . , made it clear that Vicos was a semi-feudal sort of community set in a semi-medieval society. The Vicosinos and their neighbors assumed that all human beings were by nature of different quality . . . . The Cornell Peru Project observed at the same time that modern industrial Western civilization operates largely in terms of a functionally equivalent fundamental assumption that produces very different social and cultural consequences. This is the assumption that every sane adult member of a society enjoys the right of egalitarian citizenship."

But the Project took over managerial control of Vicos and actually reinvested profits for the serfs! "No 'patron' had ever plowed profits back into Vicos."

This article and the one following it recount some of the success of the Vicos project.

5712. HUNTER, John M. Emerging Colombia. Washington, D.C.: Public Affairs Press, 1962. 116 pp. Bibliography.

Written by an economist who has had vast experience working in other nations, the book reads like a socio-political study. It is an interesting book for the person about to go to Colombia.

5713. LEFF, Nathaniel. "Economic Development Through Bureaucratic Corruption," The American Behavioral Scientist, 8(3):8, November, 1964.

The author argues that "corruption" can be a means of allocating scarce resources in a developing nation. He presents his rather different views in a most convincing manner.

5714. *LERNER, Daniel. The Passing of Traditional Society. Glencoe, Ill.: Free Press of Glencoe, 1958.

This book is a report of extensive survey work in the Middle East during a period of rapid modernization. The Center for International Studies at MIT and Bureau of Applied Social Research at Colombia sponsored it. The introduction is by David Reisman. The book would be helpful for suggestions for questions in attitude studies.

5715. LEUTHOLD, F.O., and WILKENING, E.A. "Acceptance of New Farm Technology: A Test of a Theory of Social Interaction." Paper presented at the Rural Sociological Meetings at San Fernando Valley State College, Northridge, California, August 24, 1963.

5716. *LILIENTHAL, David E. "The Road to Change," International Development Review, 6(4):9, December, 1964.

In this abridged version of his 1964 Hillman Lecture at Columbia University, Lilienthal argues that development comes from within. He believes that "development of people is the heart of change." Four observations about change are shared with the reader. There must be faith that men can create beneficial change. Change can come quickly. There must be belief in the almost unlimited latent capacity of the average man. Finally he suggests that only new organizations or older ones redesigned can meet the needs of development.

5717. *LIPPITT, Ronald W., and WESTLEY, Bruce. The Dynamics of Planned Change. New York: Harcourt, Brace & Co., 1958. 312 pp.

"Every attempt to bring about a change at one level of unit organization raises the possibility that vested interests at other levels, external to the immediate client system (which almost invariably is a subpart of a larger system), may be threatened and might respond with coercive action."

5718. LODGE, George C. Spearheads of Democracy. New York: Harper & Row, 1962. 249 pp. Bibliography.

Although ostensibly dealing with labor, the book is an interesting polemic for the U.S. helping others help themselves make a better world.

Lodge suggests that a man will not risk his life defending what he doesn't like. It is not a question of communism and we are wrong to make this the issue. Lodge believes that the challenge is our doing a better job of change in the fields and jungles than the communists.

5719. MAIER, Joseph B. (ed.). Politics of Change in Latin America. New York: Praeger, 1964. 258 pp. Bibliographical references.

5720. MEAD, Margaret. New Lives for Old. New York: Mentor Books, 1956.

To have changed culture one must have changed adults--children will be what parents want.

Manner of education and emulation are important in determining change.

5721. *NIEHOFF, A.H., and ANDERSON, J.C. "The Process of Cross-Cultural Innovation," International Development Review, 6(3):2, June, 1964. Bibliography.

The authors draw together the results of several attempts to introduce change. Their conclusion is a hypothesis: "When a felt need and a strong practical benefit exist, along with the willing cooperation of the recipients for planning and implementation, other negative factors such as lack of awareness of local cultural patterns on the part of the innovator, lack of continuity, and non-utilization of the local economic patterns will be effectively counterbalanced."

5722. POWELSON, John P. Latin America: Today's Economic and Social Revolution. New York:

McGraw-Hill, 1964. 303 pp. Bibliographical footnotes.

5723. TUMIN, Melvin M., and FELDMAN, Arnold S. _Social Class and Social Change in Puerto Rico_. Princeton, N.J.: Princeton University Press, 1961. 549 pp. Bibliographical references.
A Social Science Research Center Study. The book is a report of a project conceived in 1952 and field work completed in 1954.

5724. TURNER, D.A. "An Analysis of Conflict and Accommodation Between Vested Interests in Eight Case Examples of Consciously Planned Social Change." Unpublished Ph.D. dissertation, University of Pittsburgh, 1959.
The newspaper in the subject city "encourages those whom it supports and discourages those whom it opposes but it does not change the convictions of anyone vitally concerned."
"Again and again the evidence makes clear that the deep convictions of persons in key positions have much to do with the formulation and shape of the plans, the nature of the conflicts and the type of solution that is secured."

5725. VAZQUEZ, Mario C. "The Interplay Between Power and Wealth," _The American Behavioral Scientist_, 8(7):9, March, 1965.

5726. WAISANEN, Fred B. "A Symbolic Interactionistic Approach to Communication and Change." Programa Interamericano de Informacion Popular, San Jose, Costa Rica, no date. (Mimeographed.)

5727. WHARTON, Clifton R., Jr. "The Economic Impact of Technical Assistance: A Brazilian Case Study," _Journal of Farm Economics_, 42:252-267, May, 1960.
This article attempts to provide

empirical evidence of the effect of technical assistance. It includes data from 82 farm families in Curvelo, Brazil, who participated in a supervised credit program for one year or more, and 49 families in Uba. Evidence seemed to indicate that the assistance had a positive effect in Curvelo. However, the assistance did not increase efficiency of Uba farms. The author has a hunch that isolation of Curvelo is one reason for the differential response to the program. Because Curvelo had had less new technology, the effect of the ACAR program was greater.

Other items that deal with Social Change are:

1103, 1153, 1157, 2010, 2014, 2015, 2601, 2807, 2902, 2904, 2905, 2910, 3013, 3103, 3105, 3121, 3129, 3133, 3207, 3213, 3406, 4102, 4103, 4108, 4109, 4902, 6001, 6005, 6007, 6013, 6014, 6015, 6023, 6024, 6601, 6603, 6605, 6606, 6608, 6614, 6615, 6618.

See also series 1700, series 5000, series 5500, and series 5800 for ideas that apply to this section.

Universitas BIBLIOTHECA Ottaviensis

5800. Attitudes

5801. COCHRAN, Thomas C. The Puerto Rican Businessman: A Study in Cultural Change. Philadelphia: University of Pennsylvania Press, 1959. 198 pp. Bibliography.

Cochran's book is another of the many studies conducted under the auspices of the Social Science Research Center of the University of Puerto Rico. In it he talks of entrepreneurship and some of the necessary conditions for economic growth. He believes that the Spanish-oriented culture has impeded economic growth.

This is not the best book ever written of attitudes and their effect on economic growth, but it is one of the few studies of this type on Puerto Rico.

5802. COHEN, Arthur R. Attitude Change and Social Influence. New York: Basic Books, 1964. 156 pp. Bibliography.

The book is an attempt to bring together and summarize much of the evidence of psychological research on the general topics of attitude change and social influence. All of the studies cited are concerned with the modification of attitudes and beliefs through communication and social interaction as well as their relevance to everyday life. The author notes differences in findings of experimental research and survey research in the field of attitude change.

5803. *"Communication and Information," International Social Science Journal, 14(2), 1962.

An entire issue devoted to communication and change of attitudes.

5804. EDWARDS, Harold T. "Power Structure and Its Communication Behavior in San Jose, Costa Rica." Unpublished Ph.D. dissertation, Michigan State University, 1963.

Methodology and conclusions concerning a community power structure study.

5805. EMERY, Frederick E., OESER, O.A., and TULLY, Joan. Information Decision and Action: A Study of the Psychological Determinants of Changes in Farming Techniques. Melbourne, Australia: University of Melbourne Press, 1958. 132 pp. Bibliography.

5806. *ERASMUS, Charles J. Man Takes Control; Cultural Development and American Aid. Minneapolis, Minn: University of Minnesota, 1961. 365 pp. Bibliography.

An outstanding book by an applied anthropologist on cultural change and the attitudes affecting that change.

5807. FAYERWEATHER, John. The Executive Overseas. Syracuse: Syracuse University Press, 1959. 195 pp.

The importance of culturally based attitudes and the view of the United States through the eyes of others is discussed.

5808. GOULDER, Alvin W. "The Norm of Reciprocity: A Preliminary Statement," American Sociological Review, 25(2):164, April, 1960.

5809. *HAGAN, Everett E. On the Theory of Social Change: How Economic Growth Begins. Homewood, Illinois: Dorsey Press Inc., 1962. 557 pp. Bibliography.

This is one of those books that has sold quite well in spite of some uncomplimentary reviews. Dr. Hagan, an economist by training, has presented some unusual views. He draws heavily upon the psychologist and anthropologist to explain economic development.

5810. HANSEN, Niles M. "The Protestant Ethic as a General Precondition for Economic

Development," The Canadian Journal of Economics and Political Science, 29(4): 462, November, 1963.

5811. *JACOBSON, Eugene, KUMATA, Hideya and GULLAHORN, Jeanne E. "Cross-Cultural Contributions to Attitude Research," Public Opinion Quarterly, 24(2):205, Summer, 1960.

An excellent review of contributions. Over fifty studies are cited in the article.

It is only one of the eight in this special issue of P.O.Q. which was edited by Daniel Katz.

5812. *JOHNSON, John J. (ed.). Continuity and Change in Latin America. Stanford; California: Stanford University Press, 1964. 282 pp.

This volume is the result of papers presented at a conference on the above subject. The conference was held in early February, 1963, under the sponsorship of the Social Science Research Center and American Council of Learned Societies, Joint Committee on Latin American Studies.

In the introduction Johnson sets the tenor, suggesting that "since World War I an endless succession of scheduled and unscheduled changes has racked Latin America . . . and one way or another, political and social reorganization is under way." Eight types of persons are looked at, then as a wrap-up the author of the final chapter compares Latin America and Japan. He suggests that Latin America offers a promising area for comparative studies. The chapter titles and the respective authors are:

"The Peasant"	Charles Wagley
"Rural Labor"	Richard N. Adams
"The Writer"	Fred P. Ellison
"The Artist"	Gilbert Chase
"The Military"	Lyle N. McAlister
"The Industrialist"	W. Paul Strassman
"The Urban Worker"	Frank Bonilla

"The University Student"	K. H. Silvert
"Latin America and Japan Compared"	R. P. Dore

5813. LASSEY, William R. "Communication, Risk, and Decision-Making." Unpublished Ph.D. dissertation, Michigan State University, 1964.

This is an account of certain aspects of a new corporation which had public subscription of its stock in Costa Rica.

5814. LAUTERBACH, Albert. "Executive Training and Productivity: Managerial Views in Latin America," Industrial and Labor Relations Review, 17(3):357, April, 1964.

5815. ________. "Managerial Attitudes and Economic Development," Kyklos, 15(2), 1962.

5816. *MERRILL, R.S. "Resistance to Economic Change: The Masai," Proceedings of the Minnesota Academy of Science, 28:120, 1960.

The Masai have rejected attempts to convert them to hunters and/or farmers. One reason is that their present way of handling their life provides higher standards for less work.

"One should not speak of people as conservative, or use of the term progressive as a personal characteristic, until it can be demonstrated that they are averse to accepted alternatives that are clearly (and by their own definition) advantageous."

5817. SPECTOR, Paul, et al. Communication and Motivation in Community Development: An Experiment. Washington, D.C.: Institute for International Services, An Affiliate of the American Institute for Research, November, 1963.

"This report describes a study in

which various communication media were used in a systematic campaign to induce people in rural communities to adopt several innovations." The experiment was carried out in relatively isolated towns in the mountains of Ecuador.

5818. RYCROFT, W. Stanley, and CLEMMER, Myrtle M. A Study of Urbanization in Latin America. Revised ed. New York: Office for Research, United Presbyterian Church in the U.S.A., December, 1963. 150 pp. Bibliography.

"This study is an attempt to describe and analyze the relatively new phenomenon of urbanization in relation to the social and economic development of Latin America." The thorough and interesting study is based to a large extent on a United Nations meeting held in Mar del Plata, Argentina, early 1963.

5819. SMITH, Thomas L. "Observations on the Middle Classes in Colombia," Materiales Para El Estudio De La Clase Media En La America Latina. VI Pan American Union, 1961. Also in Colombia, People & Institutions. Baton Rouge, Louisiana: Louisiana State University Press, 1951 (?).

Gives reasons why people at Medillin, Colombia, are different.

5820. WILKENING, Eugene A. "Some Perspectives on Change in Rural Societies," Rural Sociology, 29(1):1, March, 1964.

Other items that deal with Attitudes are:

2008, 2010, 2014, 2116, 2117, 2118, 2601, 2807, 2902, 2905, 3004, 3013, 3105, 3148, 3213, 4103, 4902, 5005, 5008, 5901, 5902, 6006, 6007, 6009, 6011, 6013, 6014, 6025, 6602, 6603, 6609, 6617, 6832, 6833, 6903

Much of series 5500 as well as series 5700 overlaps with items in this section.

5900. Bibliographies

5901. *DOBYNS, Henry F., and VAZQUEZ, Mario C. The Cornell Peru Project Bibliography and Personnel. (Cornell-Peru Project Pamphlet No. 2.) Ithaca, New York: Cornell University, 1964. 55 pp.

The first part of the booklet gives a chronology of events together with some information about primary collaborators in the Vicos project. The last part consists of a three-part bibliography of the project.

5902. HART, Donn V., and MEADOWS, Paul. "An Annotated Bibliography of Directed Social Change." Syracuse, New York: Maxwell Graduate School of Citizenship and Public Affairs, Syracuse University, October, 1961. (Multilithographed. Unpaged.)

A good bibliography of 405 references, half of which are annotated. The bibliography stresses peasant societies and it reflects an anthropological emphasis. But the bibliography has no index and is not subdivided into geographical areas or specialities, which makes it rather difficult to read.

5903. "List of Publications." East Lansing, Michigan: Communications Research Center, Michigan State University, Summer, 1963. (Mimeographed.) 23 pp.

This pamphlet annotates the publications of faculty and staff members of Communications College. Much of the work has to do with development and has not yet been published but is available free from the Communications Research Center.

5904. *ROGERS, Everett M. "Bibliography of Research on the Diffusion of Innovations." Research on the Diffusion of Innovation Publication No. 1. Department of Communication, Michigan State University, 1964.

The Communications Department of Michigan State University has published a series of bibliographies. This bibliography, a continuation of the one in Rogers' 1962 book, is probably the most complete in the field.

5905. *WHITE, Carl M., et al. Sources of Information in the Social Sciences. Totowa, New Jersey: Bedminster Press, 1964. 498 pp.

Extremely useful source book. In addition, the first chapter, "The Literature of the Social Sciences," might be especially helpful to new graduate students.

Other items that deal with Bibliographies in Communications are:

2601, 4008, 4103, 4208, 5005, 5008, 5551, 5553, 5554, 5705, 5801, 6004, 6011, 6023, 6601, 6603, 6605, 6614, 6617

In addition, note the bibliographical sections in the other chapters of this book.

CHAPTER 6 METHODOLOGY

6000 SERIES

6000. Miscellaneous

6001. *ALMOND, Gabriel A., and VERBA, Sidney. "Cross-National Research and Political Behavior: Some Considerations of Method," Chapter II in The Civic Culture. Princeton, N.J.: Princeton University Press, 1963. 562 pp. Bibliography.

This is one of the best discussions available on the problems involved in conducting cross-national survey research and it is recommended as an ideal starting place for the student. The authors discuss the problems encountered in conducting a five-nation study involving over 1000 interviews in each nation. Problems in obtaining equivalence in interviewing schedules, situations, interviewer procedure, and in overcoming the differences in the acceptability of public opinion polling as an activity are discussed and solutions illustrated from the study itself. The authors advocate the use of patterns of responses within nations to obtain equivalence in areas where it is otherwise unobtainable. Appendices include the questionnaires, descriptions of the sampling procedure used in each nation, and an excellent discussion of the limitations of significance tests in survey work in terms of their tendency to both under- and over-estimate the significance of the study's findings.

6002. *BEERS, H.W. "Application of Sociology in Development Programs," Community Development Review, 8(1):5, March, 1963.

Beers talks of the usefulness of sociology. Interestingly, this particular issue of the magazine has a bibliography of all articles published in the CDR from its inception in 1956.

6003. BOYD, Harper W., Jr., et al. "On the Use of Marketing Research in the Emerging Economies," Journal of Marketing Research, 1(4):20, November, 1964.

There seems to be little marketing research being conducted in the developing nations. Some obstacles and technical difficulties in applying marketing research are discussed.

6004. BUCHANAN, William, and CANTRIL, Hadley. How Nations See Each Other. Urbana, Ill: University of Illinois Press, 1953. Appendix A on the Problems of Meaning, Methodology, and Evaluation. 220 pp. Bibliographical footnotes.

This book reports the findings of a nine-nation study conducted primarily with survey techniques. The appendix discusses problems of translations and concept equivalence, problems of coding and tabulation, sources of biases, and problems of the utilization of inferential statistics in interpreting the data. The authors recommend extensive pretesting and central coding and tabulation as means of increasing comparability and equivalence of data.

6005. *CONVERSE, P.E. "New Dimensions of Meaning for Cross-Section Sample Surveys in Politics," International Social Science Journal, 15(1):19, 1964.

Converse emphasizes the need to distinguish meaningful and meaningless expressions of opinion, and to relate public opinion to elite decision making. On many issues the actual "opinion public" is very small, usually less than 20% of the population, and the proportion of "don't know" responses should be viewed as "the top of the iceberg where incapacity to respond meaningfully is concerned." The author feels that many investigators persist in expecting opinions from R's where they have none,and that many R's are willing to choose an alternative when specifically asked to do so, even though they have no opinion.

6006. DEUTSCHMAN, Paul J., and MCNELLY, John T. "Characteristics of Latin American Countries," The American Behavioral Scientist, 8(1):25, September, 1964.
The authors made a statistical construction of the "average" Latin American country. Through factor analysis three central indices (size, developmental level, and exports to the United States)were found to account for considerable differences between nations.

6007. DUIJKER, H.C.J., and ROKKAN, Stein. "Organizational Aspects of Cross-National Social Research," Journal of Social Issues, 10(4): 8-24, 1954.
The authors catalog types of cross-cultural comparative research and generalize about the problems peculiar to each. They also provide a case study illustrating the organizational problems involved in doing cross-national research.

6008. FRANCIS, R.G. A Social Science Research Center Study. College of Social Sciences, University of Puerto Rico, 1960.
A discussion of means and ends of science.

6009. FREY, Frederick W. "Surveying Peasant Attitudes in Turkey," Public Opinion Quarterly, 27(3), 335-355, 1963.
This is an excellent case study of research conducted in a developing country. The author details the history of the

study and follows it through chronologically, discussing each problem as it arises in the course of the study. He notes many techniques for securing co-operation of local political units, for providing probability samples, and for training and motivating interviewing teams. He describes the evolution of the instrument used and its content. He discusses the problems of interviewing in an unwritten language, Kurdish. The training procedure for the interviewers is outlined. This study was something of an administrative feat as well as one in compiling data from a probabilistic sample of villages, village elites, and Turkish rural population.

6010. GIRARD, Alain. "The First Opinion Research in Uruguay and Chile," Public Opinion Quarterly, 22(3):251-260, 1958.
The difficulties of the survey are described. These primarily involved composing the sample, choosing interviewers, and training them.

6011. ________. "Introduction" (to a series of articles on opinion surveys in developing countries), International Social Science Journal, 15(1):7-20, 1963.
The contents of the various articles in this issue are discussed in terms of the problems faced and the solutions found to them. The author details the following problem areas: sampling problems, social structural non-equivalences, public attitude toward polling, obtaining interviewers and training them, political problems, and the construction of the questionnaires. He points out that most of the problems faced are different only in degree, not in kind, from those faced in polling in one culture.

6012. HANSEN, Millard. "Training and Research in Puerto Rico," Annals of the American Academy, 285-190:110-115, January, 1953.
Why Puerto Rico is a good place to do

social research. This volume of the Annals is devoted entirely to Puerto Rico.

6013. HAYES, Samuel P., Jr. Measuring the Results of Development Projects. Paris, France: UNESCO, 1959. 100 pp.

This is the first of an intended series devoted to the services which social sciences can provide and the methods that can be most effectively applied. Hayes jogs the memory of the researcher on a number of points. It is an excellent handbook for one's personal library.

6014. HENDRY, James B. The Small World of Khanh Hau: A Study of Economic Life and the Prospects of Development in a Vietnamese Rural Community. Chicago: Aldine, 1964. 312 pp. Bibliographical footnotes.

This book is not as unrelated to Latin America as it may seem at first glance. The author has combined the tools of the anthropologist and the economist in his case study of a village of Viet Nam. Among the subjects he discusses are the resources, the marketing process, productivity of agriculture and responses to innovation. In the appendices he has reproduced his sample survey and family budget survey.

6015. HILL, Reuben. "Cross-National Family Research: Attempts and Prospects," International Social Science Journal, 14(3): 425-451, 1962. Bibliography.

Among other things, Hill discusses the problems and strategies involved in cross-national research with delicate issues. He recommends extensive knowledge of the governmental structure in the country and of the local politics of academic collaborators. The personal introduction is cited as the most helpful device in getting to authorities who can make or break a project. It is often important to so structure the theoretical presentation of the research as to involve the interest of collaborators and officials. He claims there is evidence of great variability of success of the same strategies cross-nationally. Hill discusses the construction of equivalent interviewer guides and questionnaires. He also presents novel proposals for generating data on family interaction in the presence of the interviewer.

6016. *HOLLAND, Edward P., and GILLESPIE, Robert W. Experiments on a Simulated Underdeveloped Economy: Development Plans and Balance-of-Payments Policies. Cambridge, Massachusett[s]: Massachusetts Institute of Technology Press, 1963.

This book reports a pioneering project carried out at the M.I.T. Center for International Studies, in which a dynamic national economy model was designed and a simulation of that model used for exploring some of the dynamic problems of development and testing alternative policy combinations

6017. HUEY, George H. "Some Principles of Field Administration in Large-Scale Surveys," Public Opinion Quarterly, 11(2):254-263, 1947.

This is a description of the experiences of the Morale Division of the Bombing Survey in Japan after World War II. The article describes problems of organization and administration encountered and solutions to them.

6018. JENNINGS, M. Kent. Community Influentials, The Elites of Atlanta. New York: Free Press of Glencoe, 1964. 212 pp. Bibliographical references.

This book was prompted by an earlier report by Floyd Hunter, Community Power Structure, but differs from it significantly. Merton, in "Rovere," and Stewart, in "Southtown," focus on interpersonal influence, not influence in general. "Erie County" and "Elmira" are other famous studies of interpersonal influence. Still, several researchers have suggested that studies of interpersonal influence needs be discussed in terms of an issue, for there are multiple and often competing elites. Jennings focused on occupants of major economic posts, prescribed influentials, and attributed influentials. He suggests different kinds of power: positive, veto, filter, and potential. There is no statistical analysis in the book.

6019. KAPLAN, Bert, (ed.). _Studying Personality Cross Culturally._ Evanston, Ill.: Row, Peterson & Co., 1961. 687 pp. Bibliography.

6020. LINDZEY, Gardner. _Projective Techniques and Cross Cultural Research._ New York: Appleton-Century, Crofts, Inc., 1961. 330 pp. Bibliography.

6021. _Market Research in International Operations._ (American Management Association Management Report Number 53.) New York, 1960. 88 pp.
The seven articles in this booklet deal with tools, techniques and organizational approaches.

6022. ROKKAN, Stein. "The Comparative Study of Political Participation: Notes Toward a Perspective on Current Research," in _Essays on the Behavioral Study of Politics._ Austin Ranney (ed.). Urbana, Illinois: University of Illinois Press, 1962. 251 pp. Bibliographical footnotes.
This essay is devoted to the probabilistic study of micro-political entities and contains extensive notes and references. The history and current practices of research in micro-politics are outlined, a catalog of political typologies and orders of comparison are presented, and a variety of charts and figures outline a theoretical position on comparative analysis.

6023. RUDOLPH, Lloyd, and Susanne H. "Surveys in India: Field Experience in Madras State,"

Public Opinion Quarterly, 22(3):235, 1958.
The article examines some assumptions underlying survey research generally which may be challenged in developing nations. Issues discussed include: is the unit of opinion the individual, and does this kind of research merit support from governmental officials? It was found that a great many people had no opinion on an issue in the sense that they were unaware of any other possible position than their own. An interesting set of anecdotes about problems faced and their solutions is interwoven into this article.

6024. WALLACE, David, et al. "Experience in the Time International Survey," Public Opinion Quarterly, 12(4):708-721, 1948.
This is a collection of four short papers on a ten-nation survey. Stern deals with the clear description of the sampling universe, translation problems, and the problems of timing. Cross-nationally, it is hard to equate strata on anything other than sex and age because the significance of various other criteria differ across cultures. Bariou concentrates on translation problems and Ylvisaker on the need for prior cooperation with all the nations. She believes that all those involved should have a voice in the interpretation of findings, and that advance decisions should be cooperative. Wallace emphasizes that if the study were done again, they would request more time for preparation, abandon the desire for identical questions, bring the cooperating agencies together for meetings, and pretest thoroughly.

6025. *WARD, Robert E. Studying Politics Abroad, Field Research in the Developing Areas. Boston: Little, Brown and Company, 1964. 245 pp. Bibliography.
This excellent book, to which seven persons contributed, is an outgrowth of the work of the Committee on Comparative Politics of the Social Science Research

Council. The book should be helpful to most every social scientist working in another culture. The chapter titles give an understanding of what the book is and the range of material covered. A sampling of those titles is: "The Developing Areas: Problems for Research," "The Research Environment," "Common Problems in Field Research," Survey Techniques," and "Research Design."

6026. WUELKER, Gabrielle. "Questionnaires in Asia," _International Social Science Journal_, 15 (1):35-47, 1963.

The author discusses results and insights stemming from experience with over thirty public opinion surveys in Asia. Problems of questionnaire drafting, sampling, language translation, political permission, lack of a frame of reference for sampling control, forbidding climate and topography, and the interference of religious feasts and holidays are all discussed.

Other items that deal with Miscellaneous are:

1101, 1105, 1202, 1203, 1204, 1705, 1706, 1714, 2008, 2009, 2010, 2011, 2017, 2108, 2118, 2601, 2602, 2603, 2604, 2801, 2802, 2808, 2905, 2908, 2909, 3002, 3011, 3013, 3104, 3105, 3109, 3110, 3113, 3114, 3119, 3121, 3128, 3137, 3141, 3147, 3148, 3149, 3150, 3405, 3406, 3411, 3901, 4107, 4113, 4204, 4212, 4905, 5002, 5504, 5505, 5509, 5510, 5512, 5522, 5561, 5562, 5563, 5708, 5710, 5721, 5725

Note series 3200 for a number of items that impinge upon this section.

6600. <u>Methodological Issues</u>

6601. ADIS-Castro, Gonzalo. "A Study of Selected Personality Dimensions by Means of the Questionnaire Method in a Latin American Culture." Unpublished Ph.D. dissertation, University of California, 1957. 100 pp.

The author addresses himself to the problem of using a given psychological test in different cultures. It has been argued that since language is in itself a manifestation of cultural differences, psychological instruments which rely heavily on verbal stimuli are apt to prove invalid in cross-cultural application. This thesis is the report of the results of giving the California Psychological Inventory to five different social groups of Costa Ricans. Adis-Castro found "a fairly close correspondence in the mean scores obtained on the four scales by Costa Rican and comparable samples in the United States."

6602. BLALOCK, Herbert M. <u>Causal Inferences in Non-experimental Research</u>. Chapel Hill, North Carolina: University of North Carolina Press. 200 pp. Bibliography.

"This short book represents an effort to pull together materials on causal inferences that are widely scattered in the philosophical, statistical, and social science literatures." The author tried (and to a great extent was successful) "to sort out those ideas which seem to be most useful to the practicing social scientist who must somehow or another make sense out of his data."

A knowledge of applied statistics through mutiple regression is assumed, but all discussions are in verbal terms.

The key points from the entire book are summarized in the last sixteen pages.

6603. DOBYNS, Henry F. <u>The Social Matrix of Peruvian Indigenous Communities</u>. (Cornell Peru Project Monograph.) Department of Anthropology, Cornell University, 1964. 142 pp. Bibliography.

Dobyns notes both the success of the Cornell Vicos Project of guided social change and the numerous community anthropological studies that have been carried forward. In this monograph he discusses a method and the results of that method to get a better idea of social reality for the use of decision makers.

6604. DOOB, Leonard W. "The use of Different Test Items in Nonliterate Societies," Public Opinion Quarterly, 21(4):499-504, 1958.

Doob investigated whether different items from presumably the same behavior area yield similar scores in nonliterate societies. He found evidence that the use of a single type of item to characterize a group may easily give a misleading impression as the groups are compared cross-culturally on the basis of that item. Items can establish differences within societies, but he recommends the use of a number of indices and their patterns for comparisons among societies.

6605. FIRTH, Raymond W. Malay Fishermen: Their Peasant Economy. London: Kegan Paul, Trench, Tubner and Co. Ltd., 1946. 354 pp. Bibliography.

A detailed study of the economic structure of a Malay fishing community. The method of approach involves a "fusion between the theoretical apparatus of the economist and the field techniques of the anthropologist."

6606. GETZELS, Jacob W., and WALSH, John J. "The Method of Paired Direct and Projective Questionnaires in the Study of Attitude Structure and Socialization," American Psychological Association, Psychological Monographs General and Applied, No. 454 (Washington), 72 (1), 1958. 30 pp. Bibliography.

They claim to have bridged the gap between the two methods.

6607. GRILICHES, Zvi. "Research Costs and Social Returns: Hybrid Corn and Related Innovations," Journal of Political Economy, 66: 419, October, 1958. Also reprinted in Eicher and Witt, Agriculture in Economic Development, 1964.

6608. HOFFMAN, Michel. "Research on Opinions and Attitudes in West Africa," International Social Science Journal, 15(1):59-69, 1963. Bibliography.

This describes a variety of sampling procedures used to obtain data in several studies in West Africa.

6609. JONES, Emily L. "The Courtesy Bias in Southeast Asian Surveys," International Social Science Journal, 15(1):70-75, 1963.

Techniques are considered for overcoming and turning to good stead the cultural tendency toward extreme courtesy toward strangers and travelers in southeast Asia. These solutions involve questionnaire design (obviously pleading questions must be eliminated), the role of interviewers and their intentions and relations to the respondents, the relationship of the sponsoring agency to the field work, and the use of middlemen to introduce interviewers and respondents. In addition to considering the courtesy of respondents, the bias introduced by the courtesy and helpfulness of interviewers must be dealt with and the difficulties of low status interviewers in dealing with high status respondents and vice versa need attention.

6610. KORNHAUSER, Arthur. "The Problem of Bias in Opinion Research," International Journal of Opinion and Attitude Research, 1(4):1-16, 1947.

Kornhauser focuses on high-level biases, those coming from supervisors and theoreticians. He cites examples of bias in terms of selection of issues and the balance of questions in an interview. This article is instructive because the examples cited are not easily detected as biased, and Kornhauser makes his points clearly.

6611. *LASSWELL, Harold D. "The Emerging Policy Sciences of Development: The Vicos Case," The American Behavioral Scientist, 8(7):28, March, 1965.

A most interesting and thought provoking article. Dr. Lasswell suggests that societies mobilize intellectual resources to meet what is perceived to be the great and continuing problems of the age. He suggests that national and world insecurity is a continuing problem and that "the policy science orientation is problem-oriented . . . (and that) the policy sciences use policy for knowledge and knowledge for policy."

6612. LIPPITT, Vernon G. Determinants of Consumer Demand for House Furnishings and Equipment. Cambridge, Mass.: Harvard University Press, 1959. 172 pp. Bibliography.

Lippitt's book is one of the Harvard Economic Studies. It was a prize winner in 1956-57 and interestingly uses analysis of variance techniques for aggregating consumer expenditure data. The study is more interesting for its methodology than its findings.

6613. PARSONS, Talcott, and SMELSER, Neil J. "A Sociological Model for Economic Development," Exploration in Entrepreneurial History, 8:181-204, April, 1956.

6614. PESEK, Boris P. "Economic Growth and its Measurement," Economic Development and Cultural Change, 9(3):295-315, April, 1961.

He discusses five different methods of calculating growth rates and the algebraic parameters on which each method is based. Pesek then offers two new methods for economists to use in calculating economic growth. He also demonstrates the results of different methods by examining some actual data.

6615. ROTHMAN, Stanley. "The Lamentable Side of Researching in Chile," The American Behavioral Scientist, 8(1):18, September, 1964.

6616. ROTWEIN, Eugene. "On the Methodology of Positive Economics," Quarterly Journal of Economics, 73(4):554, November, 1957.
This is an answer to Friedman's essay, "The Methodology of Positive Economics," in Essays in Positive Economics, where Friedman argues that he is concerned only with results. If business acts "as if" and arrives there, fine. Friedman is concerned with prediction in the theory only. In essence, Rotwein believes Friedman lacked precision.

6617. "Sociology of Development in Latin America," International Social Science Journal, 15 (4), 1963.
The entire issue is devoted to issues of development.

6618. WHARTON, Clifton R., Jr. "Processing Underdeveloped Data from an Underdeveloped Area," American Statistical Association Journal, 55:23-31, March, 1960.
Problems of data handling and how to deal with them.

6619. WILSON, Elmo. "Adapting Probability Sampling to Western Europe," Public Opinion Quarterly, 14(2):215-223, 1950.
The advantages of surveying in Europe include the availability of lists of inhabitants by residence and fewer callbacks for not-at-homes. A number of sample designs are detailed to cope with specific problems of sampling in a number of European countries. He recommends a flexibility of approach to gain comparable data cross-nationally.

6620. ________, and BONILLA, Frank. "Evaluating Exchange of Persons Programs," Public Opinion

Quarterly, 19(1):20-30, 1955.
A series of experimental designs used to gather information about the effectiveness of an ongoing program of international exchange is described. Useful hints about the solution of problems through certain modifications of the panel technique are suggested in the article.

6621. ZARKOVICH, S.G. Sampling Methods and Censuses. Vol. 1: Collecting Data and Tabulation. Rome: Food and Agriculture Organization, 1961.
This is a how-to-do-it book, designed primarily for workers in developing countries who are being instructed in census taking and/or surveys. There are numerous illustrations of work that is going on and the kind of problems one runs into when doing censuses.

Other items that deal with Methodological Issues are:

1101, 1704, 1705, 1706, 1709, 2001, 2003, 2008, 2017, 2101, 2102, 2104, 2105, 2604, 2607, 3014, 3105, 3111, 3148, 3149, 3221, 4107, 4113, 4208, 4212, 4213, 4216, 4902, 4905, 5002, 5011, 5014, 5508, 5509, 5511, 5552, 5555, 5562, 5563, 5706, 5711, 5712, 5721, 5804, 5819, 5901, 6001, 6003, 6604, 6005, 6008, 6010, 6011, 6015, 6016, 6019, 6020, 6021, 6022, 6024, 6026

See series 6810 and series 6900 also.

6810. Interviewers and Interviewing

6811. FINK, Raymond. "Interviewer Training and Supervision in a Survey of Laos," International Social Science Journal, 15(1): 21-34, 1963.

This is a case study detailing the problems of quickly getting a questionnaire into the field with inadequate bilingual assistance. A six-stage translation system involving three languages had to be used. The author describes his training program for interviewers, the problems faced in sampling and in supervising interviewers, and other aspects of his study. Generally he recommends leaving very little to the judgment of helpers in a cross-cultural survey, at least when they have little training in social science.

6812. RADVANYI, Laszlo. "Problems of International Opinion Surveys," International Journal of Opinion and Attitude Research, 1(2):30-51, 1947.

This is a rather inclusive survey of types of problems encountered in cross-national opinion surveys. Included are the problems of meaning equivalence, differing attitudes toward polling as an activity, sampling problems, and interviewer selection and training. Much of the article is devoted to the latter issue and the point is made that contact and control are imperative. The author also reports evidence that non-paid interviewers cheat less, at least in Latin-American countries.

6813. REH, E. Manual on Household Food Consumption Surveys. (Nutritional Studies, No. 18.) Rome: Food and Agriculture Organization, 1962.

A how-to-do-it manual for researchers interested in determining food consumption.

6814. STYCOS, J. Mayone. "Further Observations on the Recruitment and Training of Interviewers in Other Cultures," Public Opinion Quarterly, 19(1):68-78, 1955.

The author describes the training course for Puerto Rican interviewers working with a questionnaire on fertility. In two weeks they went through readings, lectures, discussions, practice interviews before the group, demonstration interviews, small group practice, trial interviews in the field, and private discussions. The author concluded that extensive training may do more to build morale than it contributes to professional interviewing. The training is essential if interviewers are to be flexible in dealing with new situations, willing to work under difficult conditions, and in order to give the interviewers the sense of professional status needed to do a good job.

6815. ______, "Interviewer Training in Another Culture," Public Opinion Quarterly, 6(2): 236-246, Summer, 1952.

The report of one researcher's experience in training Puerto Rican interviewers.

6816. WILSON, Elmo. "Problems of Survey Research in Modernizing Areas," Public Opinion Quarterly, 22(3):230-234, 1958.

Wilson discusses problems of sampling, interviewer selection and training, establishing rapport, and reliability and validity. He also brings attention to the fact that large masses of people have no opinion on many issues and that to require interviewers to work with these people is wasteful, hard on interviewer morale, and not justified by a desire for comparable results in several nations. Attention to the sampling of significant publics often makes better sense than a national probability sample.

6817. ______, and ARMSTRONG, Lincoln. "Interviewers and Interviewing in India," International Social Science Journal, 15(1):48-58, 1963.

The authors discuss in detail the selection of staff from various strata and the training of interviewers in a variety of approaches. The need to train interviewers to teach respondents how to respond is emphasized.

6818. YOUNG, Frank W. and Ruth C. "Key Informant Reliability in Rural Mexican Villages," Human Organization, 20(3):141-148, Fall, 1961.

Other items that deal with Interviewers and Interviewing are:

3107, 3108, 3109, 3110, 3133, 3134, 3155, 5804, 6001, 6005, 6007, 6010, 6011, 6015, 6016, 6019, 6020, 6021, 6022, 6024, 6901, 6902, 6904, 6905

See series 6600, series 6830, and series 6870 also.

6830. Problems of Equivalence

6831. CAMPBELL, Angus, and ROKKAN, Stein. "Norway and the United States," International Social Science Journal, 12(1):69-99, 1960.

A portion of this article on comparative voting behavior in the U.S. and Norway deals with the design of comparative analysis in survey research. The authors recommend a focus on second-order comparisons of differences as lending more successfully to equivalence between nations. They further recommend that comparisons be made primarily on the basis of patterns of relationship rather than solely on the basis of statistically significant differences.

6832. DUIJKER, H.C.J. "Comparative Research in Social Science with Special Reference to Attitude Research," International Social Science Bulletin, 7(4):555-566, 1955.

The author deals with fundamental issues underlying the effort to attain equivalence of measurement. He discusses the meaning of equivalence conceptually and discusses the problems faced in establishing it in sampling, language, and interviewing situations. This is an excellent and useful article.

6833. JACOBSON, Eugene. "Methods Used for Producing Comparable Data in the OCSR Seven-Nation Attitude Study," Journal of Social Issues, 10(4):40, 1954.

The measures included pretesting, conferences and translation for functional equivalence of instruments in terms of content, order, and context. The total process of questionnaire translation, interviewer selection and training, coding and data preparation, the coordination of analysis, and the division of labor is outlined.

Other items that deal with Problems of Equivalence are:

3104, 3105, 3112, 4212, 5012, 6001, 6004, 6005, 6007, 6009, 6015, 6021, 6024, 6025, 6901, 6902, 6904, 6905.

See series 6600, series 6810, and series 6870 for other items of use here.

6870. Translation Problems

6871. *CASAGRANDE, Joseph B. "The Ends of Translations," International Journal of American Linguistics, 20(4):335-340, 1954.
This is the classic discussion of translation problems, not only for surveys, but in all activities requiring interpreters. One of Casagrande's main points is that it is necessary to translate CULTURES, not merely words or phrases, for equivalence in any meaningful sense.

6872. ERVIN, Susan, and BOWER, Robert T. "Translation Problems in International Surveys," Public Opinion Quarterly, 16(4):595-604, 1953.
This is a good discussion of the problems of meaning and the kinds of meaning difficulties faced in translation. The authors discuss distortions arising from differences in word meaning, in syntactical context, and in cultural context. The problem of dialects is also discussed.

6873. PHILLIPS, H.P. "Problems of Translation and Meaning in Field Work," Human Organization, 18(4):184, 1959. Bibliography.
This is an exhaustive discussion of the language difficulties of a cultural anthropologist with examples from the author's work in Thailand. The focus is on translation problems in primitive cultures. There is a valuable discussion of the effect of the interpreter on the interview between anthropologist and respondent. A variety of translation techniques are discussed and certain concepts are tagged as untranslatable. A list of instructions for translators together with cautions for their use is included.

6874. STERN, Eric, and D'EPINAY, Rene L. "Some Polling Experience in Switzerland," Public Opinion Quarterly, 11(4):553-557, 1947.
The authors describe their approach to

multilingual polling and the problems raised by the persistence of local dialects which had to be used to secure rapport.

Other items that deal with Translation Problems are:

5807, 6004, 6009, 6010, 6011, 6024, 6025, 6901, 6902, 6904

See series 6600, series 6810, and 6830 for other items of use here.

6900. Bibliographies

6901. HASTINGS, Philip K. "The Roper Public Opinion Research Center: International Archive of Sample Survey Data," International Social Science Journal, 16(1):90, 1964.

Elmer Roper and Associates deposited the results of much of their survey work at Williams College in Williamston, Massachusetts. In addition, the code books and master card deck for a number of other studies are on file. The services of the Center are available (as are the ones at Berkeley's data book ;see item 6903) to scholars throughout the world.

6902. Input-output Bibliography 1960-1963.(Statistical Papers, Series M, No. 39.) New York: United Nations, 1964. 159 pp.

This is a supplement to the 1961 bibliography by Taskier. See item 6906.

6903. MITCHELL, Robert E. "The Survey Research Center University of California Berkeley," International Social Science Journal, 16(1):86, 1964.

The International Data Library and Reference Service was established by the Survey Research Center and the Institute of International Studies to assist social scientists in obtaining, processing and analysing existing survey materials from throughout the world. Their services are available to interested scholars at other universities.

(See International Social Science Journal, 16(3):434, for later article on the same subject.)

6904. ROKKAN, Stein. "Comparative Cross National Research: Bibliography," International Social Science Bulletin, 7(4):622-641, 1955.

This is quite a large and exhaustive bibliography subdivided into subject headings. Of most interest to survey research are the following:

- Problems of Method and Organization:
  - Data Gathering and Data Categorization--28 items
  - Problems of analysis and inference--11 items
  - Translation Problems--11 items
- Comparisons Based on Sample Surveys and Opinion Polls:
  - Problems of Comparability--33 items

6905. ________. "Introduction. The Use of Sample Surveys in Comparative Research," International Social Science Journal, 16(1):7-18, 1964.

Rokkan discusses the history of sample surveys and attributes accelerating developments to the proliferation of local survey agencies around the world and the growth of machine processing of data. He also reports that UNESCO has taken on the project of preparing a series of guides and manuals for research workers in this area of sample surveys in comparative work.

6906. TASKIER, C.E. Input-Output Bibliography, 1955-1960. New York: United Nations, 1961. 222 pp.

This comprehensive bibliography was produced by the United Nations through special arrangements with the Harvard University Economic Research Project. The 600 item bibliography is a follow-up to an earlier publication, Bibliography of Interindustry Economic Studies, by V. Riley and R.L. Allen, published by Johns Hopkins Press, 1955.

Other items that deal with Bibliographies are:

1105, 1704, 1706, 2010, 2011, 2602, 3105, 3148, 3149, 3221, 4107, 4113, 4212, 4905, 5002, 5014, 5721, 5725, 5804, 6621, 6831, 6832, 6833, 6871, 6872, 6873

Note the bibliographical sections in the other chapters. See also Series 6000.

APPENDIX A

OTHER SOURCES OF INFORMATION

In preparing this bibliography I have become quite impressed with the amount and quality of already published material. However, it seemed to take so much time and effort to find out about good sources. In this section, I will attempt to make the job easier for those interested in fields covered by this bibliography who may not already be familiar with all the numerous source documents. To accomplish this goal,I have used two different methods.

First of all, each chapter has a bibliography section that lists those documents and agencies,I found most helpful. In addition, I am listing here in this separate section some additional reference sources that might also be considered by the serious student.

To Find Books

In addition to the regular card catalogue and personal help from your librarian, there are three other places I would suggest looking when trying to find books.

1. Earl J. Pariseau (ed.) Handbook of Latin American Studies. There is a new version of this book every year. It is, simply stated, an annotated bibliography organized by subject area. (See item 2910 in text.)

2. Books in Print. Published annually by the R.R. Bowker Co. of New York, this book lists those books by author, title and subject that have been noted in the Trade List Annual. This publishing company has just begun publishing another reference book. It is called Libros en Venta.

3. Libros en Venta aims to provide complete information, including price and source, for all books currently available from book publishers of the Spanish-speaking world. Here, too, books are listed by author, title, and subject.

To Find Abstracts and Indexes to Articles and Statistics

In addition to the most common sources of information such as Readers Guide and Public Affairs Information Service, the scholar or researcher interested in some areas covered in this bibliography might find it worth his time to check the following information sources.

4. World Agricultural Economics and Rural Sociology Abstracts. This periodical as of 1965 is in its seventh year of publication. As the name implies, articles from various nations are abstracted. It is now published by the Commonwealth Agricultural Bureau of Farnham Royal, Bucks, England.

5. Statistical Theory and Methods Abstracts. This is a multilithed journal of the International Statistical Institute. It is published in the British Isles (by Oliver and Boyd of Edinburgh, Scotland.) The Journal has one of the most sensible organizations for an abstract that I have seen. It is set up so that it can be easily cut apart and made into index cards. In addition each major area is printed on a certain color of paper. In the introduction there is a note that "The aim of this journal of abstracts is to give complete coverage of papers in the field of statistical theory and new contributions to statistical method."

6. International Information Service Quarterly. This handbook was formerly known as The World in Focus. It is published by the Library of International Relations in Chicago. It attempts to provide a guide to documentary sources, scholarly analyses, and significant commentaries on contemporary political, economic and social developments in all parts of the world.

7. The International Executive. This periodical always includes a number of abstracts of articles that may be of interest to the busy executive who is concerned with events other than those in the United States.

8. A Guide to Current Latin American Periodicals. This book, which was published in 1961 by Kallman, was compiled by Irene Zimmerman. It contains a wealth of information about periodicals of Latin America. The author takes several different approaches in presenting her material. This redundancy makes it much easier for the reader to find needed information.

9. UNESCO International Committee for Social Sciences Documentation (ed.), _International Bibliography of the Social Sciences_. Chicago: Aldine.

This international bibliography consists of four annual volumes which cover sociology, anthropology, political science, and economics, respectively. These bibliographies cover material of the two previous years. They should be quite useful for the social scientist because of their comprehensive subject and author indexes.

Organizations Having an Interest in Development

10. Gale Research Company of Detroit, Michigan published a number of reference books. Of special interest to the reader might be the following books which most large city and university libraries have on their reference shelves.

(a) _The Developing Nations: A Guide to Information Sources Concerning Their Economic, Political, Technical, and Social Problems_.

(b) _Directory of Special Libraries and Information Centers_.

(c) _Statistics Sources_.

(d) _Research Centers Directory_.

(e) _Book Review Index_.

11. United States Government. Each month the Superintendent of Documents publishes the _Monthly Catalogue of U.S. Government Publications_. The catalogue is a veritable treasure house of free or low cost information. The Departments of Agriculture, Commerce, Labor and State all are contributing numerous works in the area of economic development.

In addition, the External Research Staff of the U.S. Department of State publishes annual booklets entitled _Studies in Progress_.[1] There are seven separate booklets, one for each of six geographical areas around the world and a seventh for the area of International Affairs.

The Bureau of Intelligence and Research, External Research Staff (INR/XR) at the U.S. Department of State wishes to know of studies that are

---

[1]Until this year (1965), there was also published a booklet of completed studies. According to recent personal conversations, the booklets on completed studies are no longer being published.

being conducted concerning other nations by scholars and commercial firms. Their card files of studies under way are available for perusal of interested scholars who are in the Washington area. In addition they will answer specific inquiries made by letter.

In early 1964, the Foreign Area Research Coordination Group (FAR) was established to "plan and to administer more effectively contracts in social science research." The director of the State Department External Research Staff, Mr. William J. Nagle, is also the FAR chairman. There has been a FAR Latin American subcommittee organized. At the time of this writing (April, 1965) Mr. John Evans of United States Information Agency is the chairman.

11. United Nations. This organization also puts out a periodical index--The United Nations Documents Index. So many of its documents are never published by commercial publishers but have the information that is invaluable to social science researchers. Of special interest to the reader will be some of the publications of UNESCO and FAO. These organizations are subsidiaries of the United Nations. UNESCO has an interesting series called Social Science Clearing House Documents and FAO has a series of basic studies in the Freedom From Hunger campaign.

12. The Organization of American States-Pan American Union. Like the U.S. Government and the United Nations, this organization also published an index of its material. It is the Catalogue of Publications.

13. Technical Assistance Information Clearing House of 44 East 23rd St., New York 10010, will likely be of help to persons just beginning research on any specific topic in a developing nation. The TAICH is an arm of the American Council of Voluntary Agencies for Foreign Service Inc. and operates under contract with USAID. Their specific job is keeping track of various development projects that are under way throughout the world. They especially are interested in the work of voluntary agencies.

APPENDIX B

ITEMS OF SPECIAL INTEREST

The items listed below are some of the most valuable that have been published in their fields. Each of these items is starred in the main part of the bibliography and is listed in the same order here, by item number. Here only the last name of the author and a short title are used.

STARRED ITEMS

#	Author(s)	Title
1106.	Ward,	Rich Nations and Poor
1154.	Eisenhower,	The Wine is Bitter;...
1155.	Hirschman,	Latin American Issues:...
1206.	Hirschman,	The Strategy of Economic Development
1207.	Hoselitz,	Theories of Economic Growth
1209.	Liebenstein,	Economic Backwardness and Economic Growth
1710.	Mead,	Cultural Patterns and Technical Change
2006.	Galbraith,	Economic Development
2010.	Meynaud,	Social Change and Economic Development
2101.	Adams,	Public Law 480 and ...
2114.	Powelson,	Latin America,...
2116.	Strassman,	Is Puerto Rican Economic Development a Special Case?
2604.	Ginsburg,	Atlas of Economic Development
2805.	Furtado,	Development and Underdevelopment
2808.	Schumpeter,	The Theory of Economic Development
2908.	Katz, McGowan,	A Selected List of U.S. Readings on Development
2910.	Pariseau,	Handbook of Latin American Studies

3006.	Holton,	Changing Demand and Consumption
3113.	Dewey,	Peasant Marketing in Java
3120.	Foster,	Some Domestic Agriculture Marketing Problems of Colombia
3122.	Galbraith, Holton,	Marketing Efficiency in Puerto Rico
3151.	Staley,	A Case Study of Response to Agricultural Prices
3202.	Bonnen, Eicher, Schmid,	Marketing in Economic Development
3205.	Collins, Holton,	Programming Changes in Marketing
3207.	Firth, Yamey,	Capital Saving and Credit in Peasant Societies
3209.	Hollander,	Retailing Cause or Effect
3213.	Hoselitz, Moore,	Industrialization and Society
3214.	Hoyt,	Impact of a Money Economy
3216.		Marketing - Its Role in Increasing Productivity
3222.	Rostow,	The View from the Seventh Floor
3412.	Sorenson,	Agricultural Market Analysis
3904.	Stewart, Simmons,	A Bibliography of International Business
4006.		Freedom From Hunger Campaign
4103.	Inter American Committee for Agricultural Development,	Inventory of Information Basic to the Planning of Agricultural Development
4104.	________,	Inventory of Information Basic to the Planning of Agricultural Development in Latin American, Brazil
4108.	Posada,	Economics of Colombian Agriculture
4203.	Eicher, Witt,	Agriculture in Economic Development
4204.		Factors Associated with Differences and Changes in Agricultural Produc-

		tion in Underdeveloped Countries
4212.	Schultz,	Transforming Traditional Agriculture
4213.	Stevens,	Elasticity of Food Consumption
4901.		Bibliography; Agrarian Reform and Tenure
4902.		Bibliography of the Cornell-Peru Project
4903.		FAO Bibliography of Food and Agricultural Marketing
5010.	Geiger, Solomon,	Motivations and Methods in Development and Foreign Aid
5013.	Pye,	Communications and Political Development
5501.	Barnett,	Innovation: The Basis of Cultural Change
5507.	Diamond,	Studies in Innovation Theory
5512.	Kriesberg,	Entrepreneurs in Latin America ...
5519.	Maynard,	Economic Development and the Price Level
5522.	Meyer, Walker, Letwin,	Motive Patterns and Risk Preferences
5523.		The Rate and Direction of Inventive Activity
5530.	Strassman,	Risk and Technological
5552.	Dahling,	Shannon's Information Theory...
5558.	Katz,	Studies of Innovation
5564.	Rogers,	The Diffusion of Innovations
5565.	Tax,	Penny Capitalism
5709.	Goodenough,	Cooperation in Change
5710.	Holmberg,	The Changing Values and Institutions of Vicos...
5714.	Lerner,	The Passing of Traditional Society
5721.	Niehoff, Anderson,	The Process of Cross-Cultural Innovation

5803.		Communication and Information
5806.	Erasmas,	Man Takes Control
5809.	Hagan,	On the Theory of Social Change
5811.	Jacobson, Kumata, Gullahorn,	Cross-cultural Contributions to Attitude Research
5812.	Johnson,	Continuity and Change in Latin America
5816.	Merrill,	Resistance to Economic Change
5901.	Dobyns, Vazques,	The Cornell-Peru Project Bibliography and Personnel
5904.	Rogers,	Bibliography of Research on the Diffusion of Innovations
5905.	White,	Sources of Information in the Social Sciences
6001.	Almond, Verba,	The Civic Culture
6002.	Beers,	Application of Sociology...
6005.	Converse,	New Dimension of Meaning...
6016.	Holland, Gillespie,	Experiments on a Simulated Underdeveloped Economy...
6025.	Ward,	Studying Politics Abroad...
6602.	Blalock,	Causal Inferences...
6611.	Lasswell,	The Emerging Policy Sciences of Development
6871.	Casagrande,	The Ends of Translations
6902.		Input Output Bibliography..

INDEX OF AUTHORS

together with associated item numbers

Universitas BIBLIOTHECA Ottaviensis